The Book of
Porlock

The Book of
Porlock
A Pictorial Celebration

Dennis Corner

HALSGROVE

First published in Great Britain in 1999

Copyright © 1999 Dennis Corner

British Library Cataloguing-in-Publication Data
A CIP record for this title is available from the British Library

ISBN 1 84114 039 2

HALSGROVE
PUBLISHING, MEDIA AND DISTRIBUTION

Halsgrove House
Lower Moor Way
Tiverton, Devon EX16 6SS
Tel: 01884 243242
Fax: 01884 243325
website: http://www.halsgrove.com

Printed and bound in Great Britain by Bookcraft Ltd., Midsomer Norton

Contents

Acknowledgements

Many of the photographs in this book are from my own collection, but many others have been loaned by the Dovery Manor Museum, Porlock. I thank the management committee for their permission to borrow and use them (and credit all such photographs as 'PM'). I am also grateful for the help of Mrs Lita Strampp and Mr Bruce Raidl of the museum in sorting and selecting the images.

I acknowledge with thanks the loan of slides and photographs from Don Beeson (DB), Fred Cape (FC), Mrs Mary Collins (MC), Mrs Jill Fitzer (JF), Messrs Michael Ireland (MI), Vivian Perkins (VP), David Urry (DU), Philip Weaver (PW), David Westcott (DW) and Mr and Mrs Glyn Willicombe (GW). Heartfelt thanks to Graham Haw (GH), who not only lent material but also devoted many hours to scanning all of the photographs for the book and recording them on CD. Thanks to Mrs Joan Hadley for permission to use excerpts from the late W.R. Hadley's unpublished *History of Porlock*. I am grateful for the willing help with information and advice which I have received from many residents of Porlock. Lastly, thanks to my wife and daughter for the long hours spent typing and reading the manuscript.

*Jim Powell who was the town
crier and bill-poster until the
time of the Second World War.*

Foreword

*T*he *Book of Porlock* is one of a growing number of titles to be published as part of Halsgrove's Community History Series, an ongoing project which aims to provide a lasting record of local communities over the years. The West Country is fortunate in that so many of its hamlets, villages and towns retain their centuries-old sense of place, and none more so than Porlock – a unique parish characterised by a relatively isolated situation and a concomitantly close-knit community. Little more than pack-horses went further than Porlock until the 19th century and the parish has had to rely on its own resources perhaps more than most – especially since the demise of its trading days by sea.

As a result of this, Porlock has always had, and still retains, a vibrant, bustling atmosphere. Unlike so many other small communities, it has escaped the death of the village shop, the school, the village social life and clubs, and remains an active, thriving place. The main street still advertises the trades that have long served the villagers and Porlock is just as much 'home' as it has always been.

The publication of this book will bring a great deal of pleasure to the people of the parish and to all those who have a connection with Porlock. There are few greater compliments a writer can pay than to produce a history book about the community in which they have grown up and the hard work involved in a task of this kind runs into years rather than months. Such a labour of love would only be undertaken by someone who has the deepest affection for his own roots, the people he has lived with, and the community they all share. It is a great pleasure, and privilege, to have had a small hand in bringing about the publication of Mr Corner's book.

Naomi Cudmore
Community History Editor
Halsgrove

Cutting hay at Bossington with scythes.

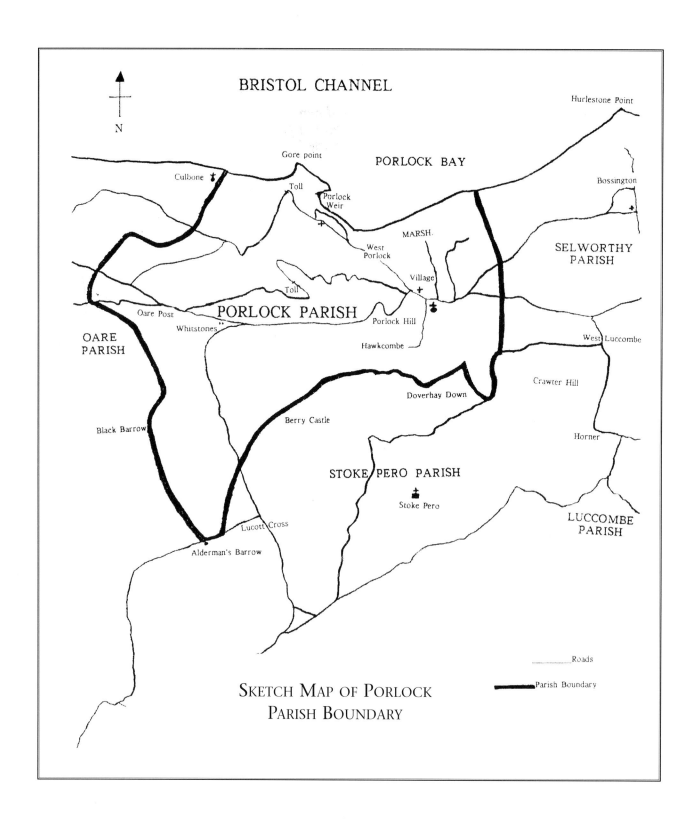

BRISTOL CHANNEL

SKETCH MAP OF PORLOCK
PARISH BOUNDARY

A Description of the Parish

The Porlock Parish is bounded in the North and North West by the Bristol Channel, on the East by the Parishes of Selworthy and Luccombe, on the South by the Parish of Stoke Pero, and on the West by Oare and Culbone. A narrow strip of land, part of the Parish of Luccombe, runs across that of Porlock quite down to the sea, dividing it into two parts, so that the inhabitants of the eastern part cannot go to their Parish Church without crossing the narrow strip above mentioned in the Parish of Luccombe. There are four Hamlets belonging to it, namely: Bossington, Yearnor, West Porlock and Porlock Weir.

This is how the parish was described during the 19th century. At this time Bossington was clearly part of Porlock Parish, but on 25 March 1884 it became part of Selworthy Civil Parish, as it is today (although it remains within the Porlock Ecclesiastical Parish). The keystone on the road bridge at Bossington bears the letters PP and SP denoting the boundary of the two parishes of Porlock and Selworthy.

Parish boundaries were set out in Saxon times, counties being divided into hundreds which, in turn, were subdivided into parishes; Porlock was part of the hundred of Carhampton. Inland parishes such as Luccombe often had strips or corridors of land which provided access to the sea. From the Domesday Survey of 1086 we learn that part of the parish of Luccombe was known as 'Doveri' or 'Dovery' (today it is generally known as 'Doverhay') and it wasn't until 1 April 1929 that Doverhay became part of Porlock Parish.

The present civil parish of Porlock is approximately 17 miles in circumference. Starting on Porlock Beach near the end of Villes Lane footpath the boundary follows a long hedge over five fields all the way to Bossington Lane, where it passes through a garden between two houses, then it turns towards Porlock to Old Lane and follows the lane to cross the Minehead road and climb up across the field to Luckbarrow near the Filter Station. From here it follows the Stoke Pero road towards Woodcocks Ley Farm, diverts across Doverhay Down, then follows along the top of the Hawkcombe woods where it descends to the Hawkcombe stream at the foot of Berry Castle Combe. It follows up the combe and passes through Berry Castle Camp and along the edge of the Lucott fields to the Exford road about half a mile north of Lucott Cross where it continues to Alderman's Barrow. From here it turns in a northerly direction to Black Barrow, thence to Weir Water and down the river to just above Robber's Bridge. It turns in a northerly direction again over Beggar's Knap, crosses the A39 about a quarter of a mile west of the Culbone Inn,

continues north easterly and then turns due east where it follows an ancient stone row (about 800 metres) to Stent Hill Tumulus. The stone row probably dates from the Bronze Age and although eight stones can now be counted, there would originally have been more, some having disappeared, probably as a result of forestry and military operations during the Second World War. It seems certain that the people who made the parish boundary used the line of the stone row as a marker. Sadly, many other stones marking the bounds of Exmoor and local parishes have also been lost over the years.

From Stent Hill the boundary follows a stream through Culbone Combe via Parsonage Farm and Culbone to the sea where it follows the high watermark back via Porlock Weir to Porlock Beach and the starting point. On Culbone Hill near the parish boundary there is an ancient stone with a wheeled cross, known as the Culbone stone (*above, DC*). Believed to be 6th century, it was probably put up as a marker pointing the way to Culbone Church. The ancient way towards Lynmouth went over this hill, the present road being further inland. The stone can be visited on foot via a specially-made footpath and there is a direction sign and information board just at the beginning of the road to Yearnor, opposite the Culbone Inn.

Also over the fence can be seen the foundations of the Army huts that housed the Searchlight Battery at Porlock during the Second World War.

Porlock
Manor Boundaries,
1709

Translation and transcript of a page from the manor court book, giving part of the proceedings of the court baron of William Blathwayt, senior, esq., father and guardian of William Blathwayt, junior, esq., 30 September 1709.

———————

And further they [The Homage] present that several tenants of Sparkhayes diverted the watercourse from its ancient course over the land of John Fry, esq., to the great damage of the tenants of this manor. Therefore each of them is to be in mercy iij s. iiis d.

And further they present that John Hole built a small wall on the land of John Sparke to his damage.

Therefore it is ordered that the aforesaid John Hole shall remove the aforesaid wall or otherwise make satisfaction to the aforesaid William [sic] for the offence aforesaid.

And further they present that the several tenants of this manor in accordance with the order made at the last Court have inspected the bounds of the manor and vivarium, and declare them to be as follows:

From the Parsons Mill to Devereux Well in Harcombe,
from thence to Sturts Foot, from thence to the foot of Berry Castle leaveing the Prior of Taunton's Wood on the left hand, from thence to Lucat Tillage, from thence to Horner River, from thence up the Water till you come to Chitchford, from thence to Oldmans Burrough, from thence to Blackburrough, from thence to Winicombs Foot, from thence down the Water to Wearth Wood, from thence to Vencombe Water to Hare Path Foot, from thence to Hare Path Head, from thence to Redicombs Head, and from thence down the Coomb as the Water Course leadeth to the Sea North.

And that all other things are satisfactory

Affeerers [assessors of fines]

Lawrenc[e] Sparke
John Phelps
Sworn

Chapter 1: Early Times in Porlock

The Anglo Saxon Chronicle which began in the year 890 was a form of historical record giving a day-by-day account of events as seen from a West-Saxon point of view. This was during the reign of King Alfred, known, because of his great ability as a king, warrior and scholar, as 'Alfred the Great'.

After Alfred's time the Danes still tried to make incursions into Wessex and sailed up the Bristol Channel in their long boats, plundering coastal areas. In the Anglo Saxon Chronicle we read that in 918 a Danish expedition started from the coast of Armorica (Brittany) during the reign of Edward, son of Alfred. The Danes ravaged the coast of Wales and penetrated into Herefordshire, but they suffered defeat. The coast of Somerset was well protected and although the Danes attempted to land at Watchet and Porlock, they were defeated in both places with great losses. Survivors fled to the island of Flat Holm, but were compelled to abandon their place of refuge due to starvation. They then sailed to Ireland where they settled near Dublin. Well over a century later the Chronicle records:

In the year 1052 Harold had landed at Porlock with nine ships, slaying many of the inhabitants, and carrying off cattle, captives and property. He then sailed round Land's End and eastward calling at various places including: Romsey, Hythe, Folkstone, Dover and Sandwich, Always seizing hostages and those ships which he found serviceable. Then he sailed up the Thames to London, but the King and all his Earls opposed them with 50 ships.

The Harold referred to was Harold Godwinson who later became the last of the Saxon kings and, as is well known, was killed at the battle of Hastings in 1066. During the reign of Edward the Confessor, Harold came to attack Porlock from Ireland, probably raising an army from amongst the descendants of those Danes which had settled there all those years before. After Hastings the Normans took over the country, but not without further resistance for a few years. Norman laws and customs were introduced, but much of the old Saxon ways remained and were improved on by the Normans. A gradual unification over many centuries occurred until both conqueror and conquered became Englishmen.

In Saxon times the Manor of Porlock was held by Algar before 1066. After the Norman Conquest, it was conferred upon Baldwin, Bishop of Exeter, who acted as Overlord. In the late 11th century it was held by Roger, son of Nigel. At this time it consisted of only 300 acres of wood and 500 acres of pasture. Three centuries later in 1366, Sir Nigel Loring, then Lord of the Manor, was granted a charter for a weekly Thursday market and three annual fairs, indicating that Porlock was by this time developing and becoming more important. That the market and fairs continued up until nearly 1900 is evident. In 1872 *Morris's Directory of Somerset and Bristol* describes Porlock as a 'Parish, a Market Town and small seaport in Williton Union'. Cattle fairs were held on the Thursday before 9 May and a large sheep fair in August and on the Thursday before 9 October.

The village, which has the A39 road running through it, is situated in a sheltered position, surrounded by hills on three sides, but exposed to the sea which is a mile away to the north. The land

The rugged West-Somerset coastline, peppered with rocks, coves and caves, was long an ideal haunt for smugglers.

runs up steeply to about 1400 feet behind the village, but is quite flat in the Vale which is only about 100-200 feet above sea level.

The older properties are in the High Street, Doverhay and Hawkcombe. A good number are still thatched, although much of the thatch has been replaced by tiles or slates. Some of the more modern houses were built between the two world wars, but most have appeared since the end of the Second World War.

The village is well served with shops, restaurants, cafés and hotels and its main industries are tourism and farming. About three-quarters of a mile along the Porlock Weir road is West Porlock, a small hamlet of about 20 houses. Further along after another three-quarters of a mile is Porlock Weir, the little former fishing port.

Left: *'Ye Olde Cottage' at the junction of Villes Lane. Tradition has it that this was the 'Spit and Gridiron', an ale house mentioned in* Lorna Doone *by R.D. Blackmore as the home of Master Pook, where Jan Ridd came 'to buy powder and shot for his long gun'. (PM)*

A view over the village, early 1900s. To the left are the Tannery buildings and beyond is the walled garden of New Place with the house and grounds behind the garden. Doverhay Place is in the centre of the photo. (PM)

A view of Hawkcombe in the early 1900s which is now obscured by the trees. (PM)

Looking down from Porlock Hill early in the 1990s. On the left is Porlock Caravan Park. The white building in the centre is the turbo generator building. Most of the houses in the centre have been built since the 1920s and New Place can be seen amongst the trees. Beyond is Bossington Lane and Bossington village. (DC)

The Gables, an old property in the Drang. (PM)

'Sea View' opposite the old school, c.1900. The fence was built by Mr Jim Powell for £15.10s. (including materials) and the bill for the work is in Porlock Museum.

Chapter 2: The Court Leet

The parish, in common with many others at the time, had a court leet which operated for many years. The leet in Porlock was a Manor Court held before the Lord or his Bailiff and they met to appoint local officials such as the ale taster and bread weigher who had to make sure of the quality of commodities. Some of the items presented in the Porlock Court from 1752-81 concerned people who had enclosed land on the common for growing potatoes; a fine of 6d. for the year was imposed. Lurban (Lowerbourne Water) was the ancient course. This was probably to decide the boundary between Porlock and Dovery. As usual, 10 shillings was spent on the Tithingman's dinner at which it was reported that the Pound and Shambles were out of repair and that Abraham Phelps was in trouble for erecting a paling fence to keep out a woman so that she couldn't attend the mill. For beating the walnut trees on the Lord's waste and carrying away the nuts, John Simons was fined £5, a penalty which seems rather harsh given that Porlock men and boys had always done so without any fear of trouble. No one was allowed to wash wool, or anything else, above the bridge, as 'it was an offence to the pot' which could bring a fine of 10 shillings. Porlock and the surrounding villages washed, dyed and spun their own wool at that time and, apart from a few wells, the only source of water was from the streams so this must have presented something of a problem.

MANORIAL ELECTION OF OFFICERS
ABSTRACT OF THE CONTENTS OF A PAGE OF THE PORLOCK MANOR COURT BOOK, 1705-17.

MANOR OF PORLOCK IN COUNTY OF SOMERSET

COURT OF THE VIEW OF FRANKPLEDGE WITH COURT BARON OF WILLIAM BLATHWAYT JUNIOR, ESQ., HELD 1 OCT. 1711 BEFORE GILES JACOB GENT., STEWARD THERE.

ESSOINS [EXCUSES]

AS APPEARS LATER

JURORS ON ASSIZE

NONE

TITHINGMAN THERE

LAWRENCE SPARKE, TITHINGMAN, COMES WITH HIS TITHING.

ELECTION OF TITHINGMAN THERE

JOAN FRANK, WIDOW, IS ELECTED TITHINGMAN, AND BY LEAVE PUTS WILLIAM ORCHARD IN HER PLACE.

JURY FOR THE LADY QUEEN:

HENRY WEBBER	JOHN NORTHCOTT)
WILLIAM RIDLER	WILLIAM STODDEN)
JOHN WEBBER	JOHN WISE)
JOHN RIDLER	ALEX. STEEVENS)
JOHN LEWRY	ROBERT HALL) SWORN
EVAN WILLIAMS	JOHN SAFFIN)
JOHN PARSMORE JUNIOR	JOHN THORN)
WILLIAM HOLSON	GREGORY JONES)
THO. WILLIAMS	WILLIAM SPARKE)
JOHN TAYLOR JUNIOR	JOHN PALMER)

RESIANTS

[NO NAMES GIVEN OF RESIANTS OWING SUIT OF COURT AND DEFAULTING]

JOHN PARSMORE APPOINTED BREAD WEIGHER OF THE MARKET FOR THE COMING YEAR

JOHN WEBBER APPOINTED LEATHER SEARCHER FOR THE FAIR

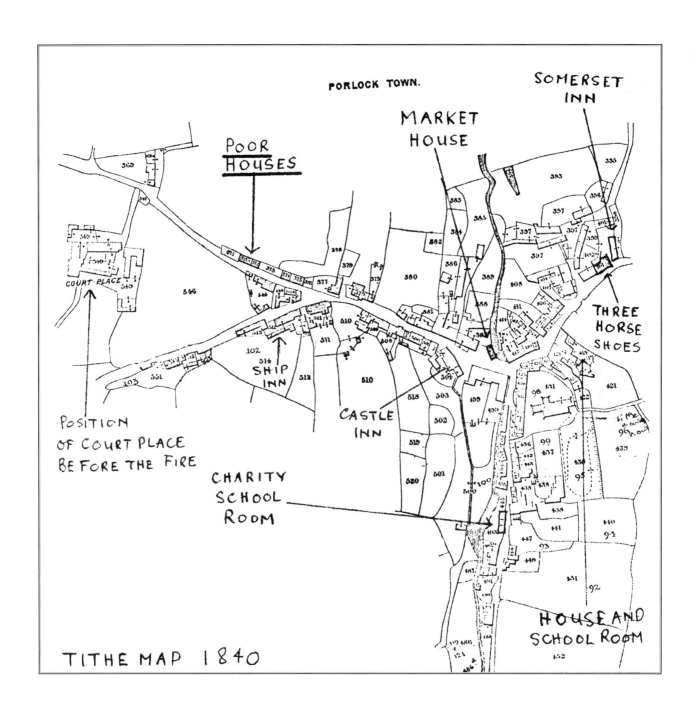

PORLOCK TOWN.

SOMERSET INN

MARKET HOUSE

POOR HOUSES

THREE HORSE SHOES

COURT PLACE

POSITION OF COURT PLACE BEFORE THE FIRE

SHIP INN

CASTLE INN

CHARITY SCHOOL ROOM

HOUSE AND SCHOOL ROOM

TITHE MAP 1840

Chapter 3: Principal Properties

The main landowners of Porlock and its surrounding area are the National Trust at Holnicote Estate, Mr Blathwayt of Porlock Manor Estate, and the Earl of Lytton of Ashley Combe Estate. Holnicote was formerly owned by the Aclands – a Devon family with its main residence at Killerton, near Exeter, but in 1944 Sir Richard Acland gave it to the National Trust. The Manor of Porlock came into the possession of the Blathwayt family in 1705, and has remained in their hands ever since. The first Blathwayt, William, was Secretary at War to James II and William III. He married Mary Winter who lived a few miles north of Bath, at Dyrham Park, where he built a fine new residence. This has been the family home for over 200 years, but has now been presented to the National Trust.

For much of the time, the Blathwayts have only used Porlock as a base for short stays but in the 19th century a widow of the 4th Mr William Blathwayt became the first family resident in the area. She remarried to one Admiral Douglas and they lived at Porlock Weir from 1824 in the house now called the Cottage Hotel. In October 1919 a later Mr Blathwayt is recorded as having a house built at West Porlock. The grounds were cleared and the gardens begun under the supervision of Mr Edward Percival, the head gardener. The gardens were filled with many flowers and shrubs from all over the United Kingdom, as well as some species from abroad, including the Tyrol and the Pyrennies. The house is now run as a hotel.

The Ashley Combe Estate once boasted a fine house. Built in 1799 it commanded magnificent views over Porlock Weir and the bay and was planted around with many rare trees. The house was built in the style of an Italian castle and there were several large tunnels in the grounds – wide enough for tradesmen's vehicles to approach the house unseen. The Lovelace family owned the house and estate which included Yearnor, Culbone, Sparkhayes and Bratton, near Minehead, and it was improved and extended at the hands of Lord King, the 8th Baron (later to become the first Lord Lovelace) who also created the Italian Gardens. The house itself was demolished in the 1960s and most of the farms on the estate have now been sold off to the tenant farmers. The present owner, the Earl of Lytton, has a residence at Lillycombe.

Another interesting property is Worthy Manor, which lies beyond Porlock Weir and is now occupied by the Hon. Rollo Clifford and his family. Records of a house on the site date back to the reign of Edward I and the estate once consisted of a farm and about 40 acres of land. Though frequently referred to as Worthy Manor, there is no evidence that it was ever entitled to be described as a manor as such. The architect, Charles Voysey (1857-1941), did much of the design work in restoring Worthy Manor, as well as buildings on the Ashley Combe Estate.

Above: *Ashley Combe House.*

Left: *Ashley Combe House with Worthy below, closer to the sea.*

Dovery Manor before its restoration in 1893/4. Note the thatched roof and the large window which has been partly covered, probably for warmth. Also just discernible are an oil lamp to the left and an outside tap – one of only 14 in the Porlock streets in the days before water was piped to the houses. (PM)

The house which stood on the site of Dovery car park until it was demolished c.1950. (PM)

Another large house of note in the area is New Place, which Sir Charles Chadwyck Healey built in the late 1800s. This house overlooks Porlock, and its entrance is at Bossington Lane. Sir Charles, who was one of His Majesty's Council and a Fellow of the Society of Antiquities, wrote *The History of Part of West Somerset* which covered the parishes of Luccombe, Selworthy, Stoke Pero, Porlock, Culbone and Oare. Published in 1901, the volume is still widely used by local history students.

Doverhay Place, which is on the Minehead road, was built at the turn of the century. A Captain/Major Perkins appears to have leased the house to tenants whilst living in London. After his death, his widow, Blanche, continued to live in the house. She later remarried and lived at Dunster Lodge, Alcombe. Doverhay Place was sold in 1932/3 to the Co-operative Holidays Association which later became the Countrywide Holidays Association. During the Second World War the house was used as a children's nursery for babies evacuated from Plymouth and it is now a private hotel.

Hacketty Way House, built by the firm of Huish's in the early 1920s for Mr Clifford, is constructed of red sandstone from West Luccombe Quarry (now disused). This lovely house enjoys a large woodland garden to the front and views over Porlock towards the sea and the hills. It is now divided into several dwellings and the former stables, coach house and gardener's cottage are private houses.

Dovery Manor stands on the site of a much older house. Although always the property of the Manor of Porlock, it is situated in the former Doomsday Manor of Dovery, later Doverhay. At one time a thatched building, it was restored in 1883-4 (and the thatch replaced with slate). During the restoration a chamfered stone base was uncovered indicating that the house was built on the site of a previous dwelling. The older house is assumed to have been built on land assigned to Isabella, the widow of Sir Simon Roges (Lord of the Manor of Porlock c.1300), as part of her dowry. The present house was probably built in the late 15th century not earlier than 1450. The hall window is unusual and closely resembles two windows in the church of Holcombe Rogus, suggesting that the same architect or builder was perhaps employed on both buildings. There was formerly a pitched court, now covered by the present roadway and foundations of older outbuildings were found opposite where there is now a car park. The property now belongs to Porlock Parish Council and is a Grade II Listed Building of Special Architectural Interest. It houses the Snooker Club and the museum which welcomes visitors during the summer months, the local residents and those who come to the area for relaxation, retirement or holidays.

Doverhay Place

Donald Hooper rounding up sheep for shearing with pony and sheep dogs. (DC)

David Westcott with his Exmoor Horn sheep, 1998. David was President of the Exmoor Horn Sheep Breeders' Society. (MC)

Chapter 4: Working the Land

The only real working farm within the village is Court Place, which has been a traditional farm for centuries. It was the site of the original Manor, and where the Manor Court was held. The farm was burnt down early in the 19th century, and the present building erected a little further westward (it being a tradition not to build on a previous site). Court Place also has the land of Holmbush on Porlock Hill and is now mainly a sheep farm.

Other farms in the neighbourhood included Sparkhayes with land stretching from the village to the sea, and Higher Doverhay Farm. All were working farms with a herd of milking cows and they flourished until the 1960s. The Sparkhayes farm is now fragmented with some of the land being used by various other farmers and other parts being developed. The farmhouse itself is now a residential home for the elderly.

Higher Doverhay still has a modest portion of land around it and is virtually a smallholding, as the fields have now either been built on or are farmed by other farmers. Crops grown in the Vale and recorded in the Bailiffs' Rolls of 1419/20 included wheat, barley, grey peas and great oats. There was a three-field cropping system where land was allowed to be fallow once every three years. The stock was mainly sheep. There were oxen for ploughing, some poultry and a few horses and pigs. In more recent times horses were used for ploughing, but during and since the Second World War tractors have largely taken their place.

Over the last 100 or so years the most noted crop in Porlock Vale has been barley which is used for malting. Porlock is famous for its barley growing and the contesting farms, including Court Place, Sparkhayes and Bossington, have won many medals and cups, not least the World Championship which has been awarded to a Porlock contestant several times.

Other former or present-day farms in the Parish are the hill farms such as Eastcott and Birchanger, Westcott, Yearnor and Ash. There is also Bromham at the top of Hawkcombe and Pitt Farm which is now a private residence as the fields have been taken over by Yearnor.

All of the farms were named hundreds of years ago and many began on a far smaller scale than has been seen during the last century. Over time, acreages increased, especially during and after the Second World War, when the requirement was to grow as much food as possible at home thereby avoiding the need for so many imports.

...d thatcher at Porlock.

Above: *Mr Moore the thatcher, c.1910. The two cottages in the picture were demolished in the 1950s to make a road to the fire station. (PM)*

Left: *Cutting reed for thatching on Porlock Marsh, winter c.1985. (DC)*

Threshing wheat at Bossington Farm. (DC)

Mr Ernest Westcott examining star oats, Eastcott Farm, 1948. (DW)

Mrs David Ridler at work in the hay field with daughter, Dorie, late 1920s. (PM)
(child's name unknown)

Haymaking at Sparkhayes Farm in the 1920s. (PM)

DOVERHAY FARMS

Top: *Farmer David Ridler senr at Higher Doverhay Farm with his wife, Elizabeth Ann, and daughters, Anne (Dorie), Clara and Sylvia. (PM)*

Above: *David Ridler junr with his sister, Sylvia, bringing sheep to their fields in Villes Lane, c.1975. The hedge on the left has now been replaced by Healey's Bungalows. (DC)*

Right: *Lower Doverhay Farm, postmarked 1907. This is now called 'Barn End'. (PM)*

DOVERHAY FARMS

Above:
*Higher
Doverhay
Farm.
(DC)*

Above: *The cattleyard of Doverhay Farm where the entrance to Hawkcombe View now is. The house to the left is now called 'Barn End', formerly Lower Doverhay. (PM)*

Left: *Farmer David Ridler harvesting. (DC)*

COURT PLACE, PITT AND WORTHY FARMS

Top: *Pitt Farm, c.1970. (DC)*

Above and above right: *Court Place Farm where farmer Mick Palmer is pictured hard at work combining. (DC)*

Right: *David Westcott and Peter Gibbons loading sheaves of oats in a field at Worthy, Porlock Weir, c.1970. (DC)*

SPARKHAYES FARM

Above, main picture: *Sparkhayes Farm House, c.1990 (DC);*
inset: *Sparkhayes c.1980. The building on the right is the old Malt House which has been converted into two dwellings. Note the vent on the roof of the building which turned with the wind, and the shuttered windows, used to maintain the right humidity for the malting process. (DC)*

Right: *George Sage going to work at the farm, 1942. (Photograph by Percy Hitchcock FRPS)*

Below: *The old cow shed and cider house, c.1950. (PM)*

Two views of the centre of Porlock taken from bedroom windows.

Main picture: *In the centre of the photograph is Cape's grocer's shop. To the right is Mr Burgess the baker's first shop which was enlarged in 1929 and next door to that is Mr and Mrs S. Stenner's newsagency and greengrocers. Further down is the shop of Mr and Mrs Noyce and next door (parallel with the two girls), the cycle shop (see opposite). (DU)*

Left: The horse and cart outside Burgess' came from Picket Stones Farm, Simonsbath (the Buckingham family) and is seen here delivering dairy produce, c.1920. (PM)

Chapter 5: Trades, Shops and Businesses

Amongst the earliest trades in the Porlock area were lime burning, charcoal making and tanning. Limestone was burned in kilns to produce lime for the building trade and for the farmers to spread on the upland fields in order to sweeten the acidic, lime-deficient Exmoor soil. The limestone was brought by boat from further up the Somerset coast, and, more especially, from South Wales. There are a few ruined lime kilns in the area, but the process died out long ago during the 1800s when larger businesses began to produce bagged lime. There is a good example of a lime kiln at Bossington Beach, as well as at Porlock Weir where a house has been built over the kiln. Other, more remote kilns, can be found along the West-Somerset coast as well as a few inland.

Charcoal burning was carried out in the surrounding woodlands, and some charcoal, together with iron ore from neighbouring areas such as Luccombe and Wootton Courtenay, was exported over the Channel to South Wales for smelting.

Tanning was a thriving industry in Porlock for several hundred years and is first mentioned at the time of James I. The Tannery became the largest business in Porlock, employing over 30 men, but closed in about 1930. The high-quality leather used for saddlery and harnesses as well as for shoes, was produced with the aid of tan obtained from the scrub oak trees, the bark of which was brought in by the cartload from the abundant woodlands around Porlock.

The parish has included quite a number of operating mills in past centuries. Some, such as Yearnor Mill, were in relatively isolated places and were no doubt used mainly by the local farmers from the hill country. Others, in the village itself, were witness to a relatively busy trade. One such was Town Mill, sited between Abbeyfield and the Castle Hotel, which is recorded as early as 1419/20. The villagers took their corn to Town Mill for hundreds of years but in 1886 it was rebuilt for the purpose of making electricity for

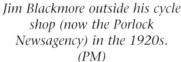

Jim Blackmore outside his cycle shop (now the Porlock Newsagency) in the 1920s.
(PM)

the Tannery. The history of Hawkcombe Mill follows a similar pattern. Once the property of the rectorial manor and used solely for the grinding of corn, it was rebuilt and then equipped in the early 1900s to generate the village's first electricity at the time when the Porlock Electricity Supply Company was formed.

While some of the mills in the parish ground flour, others, called 'fulling mills', served the local cloth industry which was still active in West Somerset around 1800. Collinson, in his *History of Somerset* (1791) describes the industry thus:

Many of the poor in Porlock are employed in the spinning of yarn for the Dunster market. The yarn made in Porlock was, according to E. J. Rawle, locally quite a famous commodity and much sought after by the cloth factors. The industry was a home-based one and some of the wives might earn as much as the man in the field.

Savage, in his *History of the Hundred of Carhampton* writes:

A considerable quantity of yarn of excellent quality was spun by hand in the parish of Porlock and its neighbourhood, which was carried to the then celebrated market of Dunster and there sold.

The shift of the woollen industry to the North of England put an end to this local employment, an event which, predictably, had a serious effect on the local standard of living.

Amongst the trade of the little harbour of Porlock Weir was the export of pit props cut from the surrounding woodlands, and imports of coal, lime and salt. The harbour was believed to have been built in 1422 and then improved a few years later. All through its history there has been a perpetual struggle to keep the narrow tidal entrance clear of shingle. A sluice and the lock gates were built in the 19th century and new lock gates installed when the harbour was re-opened in 1913. There was also a brick- and tile-making firm there during the late 1800s, the site of which is

Johnny Floyd's donkey cart – the local taxi, c.1900. (PM)

Left: *Lowerbourne House, 1920. (DC)*

Above: *The Porlock Newsagency, 1999. (PM)*

Right: *A busy street scene, 1950s. Note the prolific shrubs and creepers covering the walls of the Castle Hotel. Whilst the signs for the Central Garage are to be seen on the right, Pollard's Garage sign can be seen in the distance where Jim Pollard had his business before buying the Central Garage. (PM)*

Hawkcombe Mill

shown near the inner harbour on an Ordnance Survey map of around 1880.

The harbour itself was once famous for its oysters which were dredged in the bay. They were then 'perched' in the shallows opposite the house called 'Oyster Perch' and turned every three days. Most were sent by boat to Bristol, although some were eaten locally. Oyster shells are still often dug up in village gardens. Herring fishing was the main trade during the autumn, when thousands of herring were landed and sold to dealers (known as 'joulers'). They were then delivered to neighbouring villages and farms, and many were salted into barrels to be kept for winter food.

Of course, apart from legitimate trades, there was always a certain amount of smuggling, especially in coastal areas, and Porlock Weir was no exception. During the reign of Charles II, His Majesty's Surveyor-General of Customs visited Somerset, and on 13 June 1682 reported:

I went to Porlock, which is about four miles from Mynehead where is a very deep bay and a good harbour for small vessels, to which place there are several that belong, which trade overseas. The [preventive] officer, Richard Davis, an active young fellow, hath hitherto been paid £5 per ann. by incidents; he very well deserves £10 per ann. and be established, it being a place of trade and where great quantities of herring are taken and cured, which begets a great concourse of people and small craft, that may be of dangerous consequence to the crown unless well guarded.

During the 19th century hiding places for contraband were found near Pools Wood, in the dairy at Doverhay Farm (where there were racks and a double wall for barrels), and at Bromham Farm (which housed another 'cache' below the floor of a barn).

A list of principal inhabitants of Porlock in 1794 includes quite a number of tradesmen, indicating a healthy level of business in the village at that time:

Clergy: Rev. Brice, John; Physic: Phelps, Henry Surgeon; Traders: 2 Merchants, 2 Maltsters, 2 Linen Drapers, 1 Tanner, 1 Cordwainer, 1 Inn Keeper (Rose and Crown).

The main occupations, however, were of course farming and fishing.

It was in the 1800s that tourism began, especially with those who came for the hunting and, in many cases, stayed for the entire season. With the arrival of the railway at Minehead in 1870, and the steamers to the harbour, more visitors and day trippers began to pour into the area, first by horse bus and stagecoach, and later by motor charabancs and motor coaches as well as on hundreds bicycles and motorbikes. The hotels and guest houses prospered, and many villagers opened their homes for bed and breakfast or accommodation if they had spare rooms. Today most people arrive by motorcar, but the letting of rooms by villagers is practically a thing of the past.

Porlock is well served by its many shops, probably more so than many other West-Somerset villages but whilst the early 1900s saw the majority of the working population finding employment in the parish, many today travel much further afield to work.

The old bank, Fox and Fowlers of Wellington. (DC)

The same building in 1999, now Sanctuary Cottage. (PM)

'The Myrtles' – the shop on the left is now the Exmoor Rambler. (PM)

Samuel S. Stenner, greengrocer, delivering outside the Ship Inn, c.1920.
His eldest daughter, Vera, is holding the reins. (GH)

The west end of the village, c.1960. The fruiterer was Mr C. Westcott. (PM)

Centre of the village showing Cape's grocer's shop. (DC)

This draper's and grocery shop was also the Post Office until the 1950s. The building is now a dwelling house and the Post Office is on the left of the letter box. (PM)

John Perkin's tailor's shop was first at the bottom of Lowerbourne where there is now a hairdresser's. (PM)

The old Post Office. The shop on the right was then A. Lear, butcher, and later C. Westcott, fishmonger and greengrocer. (PM)

The Post Office, 1999. (PM)

John Ridler's Boot and Shoe Shop, c.1910. All repairs were done in the Ridlers' own workshop and John later branched out to Park Street in Minehead. Eventually his great-grandson had a sheepskin shop here. (PM)

The same building, photographed in 1987. Mr and Mrs McCoy took it over as a saddlery and leathercraft shop in 1972. (DC)

Doverhay Garage, 1934. Left: Proprietor, Frank Yeandle; right: G. James of Minehead. The Austin car was used as a taxi for private hire and for weddings and was hired by Huish's Undertakers as a hearse (with the seat removed). The garage is now Wallace Harding Car Body Repair Shop. (PM)

The Central Garage, 1920s, then owned by Jim Blackmore and Jim Bond. (PM)

PORLOCK IN BUSINESS

Left: *Mr Isaac Burgess and his son, Clifford, June 1914. (DC)*

Below left: *Sid Ward delivering with Stenner's Bakery motorbike and sidecar, 1932. (PM)*

Below: *Burgess' first shop which was enlarged in 1929. The BSA motorbike and sidecar was used for deliveries in Porlock Vale. The sidecar could also be taken off and replaced with one for private use. (DC)*

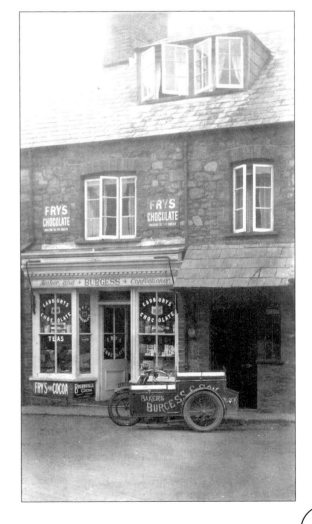

Above: *Hot Cross Bun Day at Burgess'. Leslie Corner pipes the crosses, c.1965. (DC)*

PORLOCK IN BUSINESS

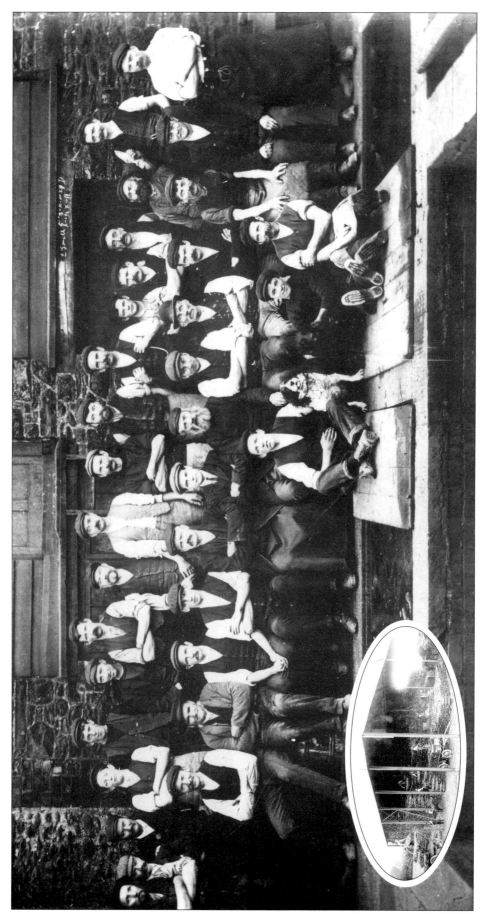

Tannery workers, 1914. Left to right, back row: Ephraim Howe, Bill Bromham, George Huish, Hedley Pocock, Jim Court, Hedley Knight, Marmie Watts, Tom Webber, Charley Yeandle, Tom Staddon, Tom Burgess, Bill Court, Ted Norman, Alf Floyd, W.I. Burgess, Jim Moore, Frank Pocock, Frank Hooper; centre: Harry Arnold, Robert Middleton, Michael Middleton, George Bushen, John Norman, Charlie Webber, William Bromham, Sidney Squire, Walter Quartley, Dave Dyer, Charley Hobbs, Fred Sedgebeer; front row: Tom Bushen, Bill Pollard, Dick Hobbs. Inset: The tannery bark shed, 1920s. (PM)

Postcard showing the centre of the village. Maria Cape's grocer's shop is on the left and Isaac Burgess' baker's is on the right, postmarked 1902. (DC)

View of Porlock High Street, c.1920. (PM)

OAK PITCHERS. OAK PALM TUBS
Made to Order

Drapery, Fancy Goods, Stationery,
Local Views.

Devon Ware. Agent for Carlton Ware.

S. G. SMITH, PORLOCK

THE PORLOCK CAFE
PORLOCK
Home-made Bread and Cakes

Devonshire
Clotted
Cream

Choicest
Butter

New-laid
Eggs
and Home-
produced
Meat direct
from our
own Farms

All Iced
Dainties

Accommoda-
tion for 150

OPEN ON
SUNDAYS

THE ALLERFORD LAUNDRY

Allerford, Minehead

ONE MILE FROM PORLOCK

High-class FAMILY LAUNDRY

REGULAR WEEKLY SERVICE
- THROUGHOUT DISTRICT
Under Proprietor's Supervision

Phone—Porlock 85.

Phone 32.

ELDEN E. ARNOLD
Grocer and Draper

THE SUPPLY STORES, PORLOCK

PRICES RIGHT,   QUALITY RIGHT,

Sole Agents for Judges' Post Cards.

POTTERY. BRASS WARE

High-grade Provisions
Dairy Produce

Films Developed at Short No
Come in, Please. Walk out F

COOKED MEATS A SPECIALITY

VICTORIA READING ROOM
Parson Street, Porlock
—:—
SNOOKER & BILLIA
OPEN TO VISITO

PARSON STREET, PORLOCK

JAMES HUISH & SONS
BUILDERS, DECORATORS, and UNDERTAKERS.
—:—
PLUMBERS, HOT-WATER FITTERS
and SMITHS.

C. H. T. BERNARD

Coal Merchant
—PORLOCK—

Stock comprises—

**COAL, COKE,
ANTHRACITE,
KINDLING,
LOGS, PEAT**
&c.

Phone—150.

D. POLLARD

General Draper
AND
Men's Outfitter

All Goods of the Highest Quality at the
Lowest possible Prices.
SATISFACTION GUARANTEED.
—:—
THE RELIABLE DRAPERY STORES
— PORLOCK —

Advertisements for local businesses, late 1920s.

C. NICHOLS & SON
HARDWARE, CHINA, GLASS MERCHANTS

District Agents for
HINTON'S CARTRIDGES & TRUMP'S
SEEDS
—:—
Fishing Tackle.   Paints, Distempers.
Wallpapers.
—:—
"ZUMMERZET" BROWNWARE A
SPECIALITY
—:—
LINO, RUGS, MATTINGS, &c.
One of the Oldest Houses in the Village.
—:—
The Myrtles
PORLOCK, Somerset

Phone 122.

T. SMITH & SON
PORLOCK

Saddlers and
Ironmongers

All requisites for
HUNTING
& SPORT

Kept in Stock.

Fishing Tackle

Permits for
Fishing issued
here.

Tel —Porlock 52

THE OLD SADDLERY SHOP

Situated in the heart of Exmoor,
we have natural access and our own
choice from the famous breed of
Exmoor Sheep and Lamb, unrivalled
throughout for high quality, tender-
ness, and rich flavour.

Post Orders receive our personal attention.

V. G. ROBJOHN
High-class Butcher
PORLOCK, Somerset

Tel. 11.

Above: *The Doverhay Forge and the work-men: blacksmiths and farriers, 1911. Jim Norman was the blacksmith followed by his son, Tom, and later Fred Kent. The bill of sale is for Floyd's Department Store, Minehead. (PM)*

Below: *Donald Bray returning a horse newly shod at Doverhay Forge. (PM)*

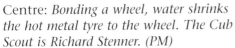

Centre: *Bonding a wheel, water shrinks the hot metal tyre to the wheel. The Cub Scout is Richard Stenner. (PM)*

Above: *Harold Rogers making a cart wheel, 1977. (PM)*

Right: *Jim Horrobin, a blacksmith who specialises in wrought-iron work, July 1999. (DC)*

An early view from the churchyard towards the old bank. (PM)

Parish Church Sunday School outing to Weston-Super-Mare, c.1960. (JF)

Chapter 6: Church and Chapel

THE CHURCH OF ST DUBRICIUS

Porlock Parish Church is dedicated to St Dubricius, formerly known as St Deveroe. Believed to have been born c.AD450, Dubricius was known to the Welsh as Dyfrig and there is a chapel dedicated to him at Llandaff, where he was Bishop of that part of the Celtic Church (which stretched from Hereford and through a great part of Wales).

St Dubricius lived to a great age, spending his later years as a hermit on Bardsey Island. He died in c.AD546 and in 1120 his remains were removed from Bardsey to Llandaff. A number of churches were probably built and dedicated to God in the name of St Dubricius, including that at Porlock which was founded by pious missionaries who travelled from across the Channel. In it a stained-glass window in the tower (erected in memory of the Revd Walter Hook) depicts the saint.

The cross-legged effigy in the arched recess in the south aisle is of a knight in chain armour of the 13th century. Traditionally, it represents a member of the Fitz Roges family, who, it is believed, were the builders of the present church.

The finest monument in the church depicts Sir John Harrington, the 4th Baron, and his wife, Lady Elizabeth, daughter of Edward Courtenay, 3rd Earl of Devon. Sir John departed for the French wars in 1417/18 and was a close supporter of King Henry V. With him went a company of 86 archers and 29 lancers, men recruited from the Porlock district. Sir John never returned and it is not known how he died, but in his will he left a long list of all his bequests which included the setting up of a 'Chantry'. Two priests were to be employed to help with the work and services of the church and to celebrate divine service and pray for the souls of Lord and Lady Harrington's parents and ancestors. It is believed that Chantry Cottage, formerly two cottages and probably the oldest dwelling in Porlock, was where they lived. The effigies are of alabaster, believed to have come from Chellaston, near Derby.

The ancient clock in the church near the tower is one of England's oldest and was taken down from the tower at the Diamond Jubilee of Queen Victoria, when the present clock was installed. It had neither face nor hands but merely struck the hour on the tenor bell. As everything was so much quieter, and the pace of life slower, men working in the fields or workshops would have heard the bell strike the hour from far and wide.

The church, 1999. (PM)

The most notable external feature of Porlock Church is its truncated spire, or steeple. The top is said to have been blown off in a gale at the beginning of the 18th century and it may be that this was, in fact, the great gale of 1703, which did great damage across Somerset, Wales and Monmouthshire. A full-scale restoration of the church was carried out during the 19th century. The spire was restored in 1884, and the oak shingles replaced. The church was closed in 1890 and services held in the schoolroom until another room had been fitted out and licenced.

On 28 May 1891 the church was re-opened by the Lord Bishop of the Diocese. All of the money for the restoration had been raised locally, and the work done by Messrs Cooksley and Huish. The parish was justly proud of the achievement of their local craftsmen. The steeple was reshingled again in 1933 using shingles of Sussex oak, 12 inches by 4 inches, which were laid like slates and fixed with copper nails.

Most of the Old Rectory was built in the early 18th century, but there is evidence that some parts are as early as 14th century. For many years the rectors held what was known as the 'Rectory Manor' and part of their living came from the rents of cottages and gardens on this land. This was predominantly in Hawkcombe and included the Mill, stretched up as far as 'Peep Out' Cottage, where the boundary turned up to Porlock Hill, thence down the road to a point near the Ship Inn, and then back to the Rectory. The Old Rectory was sold in the 1990s, and a new one built near by.

A drawing of 1839 showing the dormer window and the steps leading up on the outside to the room over the porch, now the Chapel of the High Cross. Also visible is the churchyard cross, the top of which was replaced in c.1898. (PM)

Left: *Parson Street. The building on the right was the Victoria Church Room of 1897 and the plaque is still on the wall. The upstairs room was used as a church meeting room and downstairs was the Reading Room (Billiards and Snooker Club) – later the Porlock branch of the TocH met there. Many Porlock inhabitants will remember the terrifying childhood ordeal of waiting at the top of the stairs for the school dentist. (PM)*
Right: *A recent view of the church in Parson Street from the entrance to the new school. (DC)*

Porlock Church from a postcard issued before 1897 when the new clock was installed to commemorate the Diamond Jubilee of Queen Victoria (the old clock can still be see inside the church). Note the oil lamp by the gate. (PM)

THE METHODIST CHURCH

The earliest known following of Methodism in Porlock was when Methodist ministers from Taunton first preached in the village in 1810 at the house of a widow named Mrs Sparkes, who lived near the old chapel.

Services were also held in the house which is now the Post Office. The owner, Mr Nicholas Snow, allowed the room to be used on alternate weeks with the Baptists, suggesting that there was a Baptist group in Porlock before the Methodists became established.

William Brown, founder of the Porlock building firm, could recall how Methodist prayer meetings were held secretly in an old malt house in Parson Street. He also remembered the persecution which the early pioneers suffered at the hands of other villagers. The Revd John Hensley preached from an upping-stock (mounting block) in the centre of the village in 1825 and a year later Porlock was put on the circuit map meaning that regular services were then held.

By 1832 there were 19 members of the Methodist Church in Porlock. The first chapel was built in 1837, on the corner of Sparkhayes Lane and the High Street and in place of two houses occupied by John Snow, cordwainer, and Nicholas Hawkins, labourer. The land was first leased and later bought from the Earl of Lovelace. The building opened on 25 August 1837 and seated 250 as well as providing a place for the Sunday School (started in August 1826) to gather. There were 140 scholars, a pair of supervisors and 35 teachers.

This chapel remained in use until 1927, when the Methodists transferred to their present

Celebration Arch outside the old chapel on Queen Victoria's Jubilee, 1897. (GH)

building which provided seating for 100 more worshippers than the old chapel. Porlock Methodist Church is now one part of the West Somerset Circuit within the Plymouth and Exeter District.

Left: *Methodist Youth Club and leaders on an outing to Appledore, 1948. Left to right, back row: David Marley, Ernie Pollard, Colin Cooksley, Roy Binding, Avis Ferris, Charlie Heasman, Marion Gooding, Violet Stenner, Joan Cape; centre: Leslie Ridler, Harold Rogers (behind), Alan Perkins, Peter Rice (half standing), Dorothy Ferris, Eileen Floyde, Molly Blunt, Janice Marley, Barbara Hyde; front: Clifford Glanville, Revd Neville Sutton.*

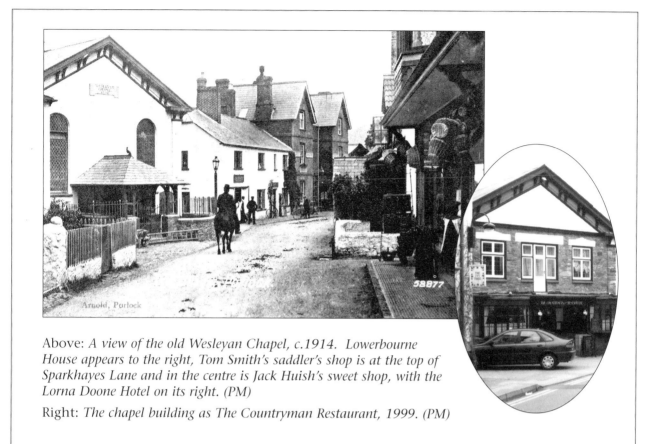

Above: *A view of the old Wesleyan Chapel, c.1914. Lowerbourne House appears to the right, Tom Smith's saddler's shop is at the top of Sparkhayes Lane and in the centre is Jack Huish's sweet shop, with the Lorna Doone Hotel on its right. (PM)*

Right: *The chapel building as The Countryman Restaurant, 1999. (PM)*

Porlock Methodist Sunday School Anniversary, c.1950. (PM)

METHODIST CHAPELS

PORLOCK, SOMERSET.

To Builders.

PERSONS DESIROUS OF UNDERTAKING THE

ERECTION

OF A

New Chapel,

ARE REQUESTED TO APPLY TO

MR. GEO. RAWLE,

OF PORLOCK,

Who will shew the proposed Site, Plan, and Specifications; and will receive Tenders for the same until SATURDAY the 18th Day of February next.

PORLOCK, 30th January, 1837.

Whitehorn, Printer, Watchet.

Left: *The contract for building the original Wesleyan chapel in Porlock was put out to public tender on 30 January 1837. It was to be in use for almost 90 years before the foundations were laid for a new building (below).*

STONE LAYERS
WESLEYAN CHAPEL PORLOCK.

Above and left: *The day of the foundation-stone laying for the new chapel which was built of red sandstone (from West Luccombe Quarry and given as a gift by the Acland family of Holnicote) and faced with stone from Ham Hill near Montacute. (PM)*

METHODIST CHAPELS

Left: *The new Wesleyan Methodist Church, 1927, designed by Mr Tamlyn, a Minehead architect, and constructed by a Porlock Methodist family, Brown Bros (below), at a cost of £4600. At the opening, the interior had not been completed – as the notice reads, 'Services in the Village Hall'. The upping-stock (mounting block) was used by the postmaster who did not want it removed but his wishes were ignored – Council workmen came in the early morning and removed it before he was out of bed!*

Above: *The opening of the new chapel in 1927. The worship area with seating for 350 was filled to capacity and extra chairs had to be put in the aisles to seat the 400 people who attended. Some £970 was raised during this one evening.*

Porlock schoolchildren, c.1900. Left to right, back row: Harry Snell, Noah Pollard, Archie Westcott, Charlie Hawkins, Perc Hobbs, Sid Smith, Charlie Perkins, Ted Huish, Herbert Ward, Jack Huish;

5th row: Wilson Whitticker, Archie Hobbs, Frank Stenner, Bill Dyer, Clifford Perkins, ?, Tom Cooksley, Sam Rawle, Hedley Pocock, Wilfred Hobbs, Ewart Perkins, Sid Huish, Fred Yeandle, Mr Brooks (headmaster), Miss Bartlett;

4th row: Mabel Bromham, Kitty Holloway;

3rd row: Governess Arnold, Effie Snell, Nancy Whitticker, Edith Rawles, Bessie Middleton, Alice Rexworthy, Honor Perkins, Maude Arnold, Annie Harding, Elsie Warner, Lizzie Ridler, Mary Dyer, Ethel Fisher, Nellie Fowler, Lizzie Bond, Queenie Whitticker, Birdie Pocock;

2nd row: Bob Bushen, Dorcus Pollard, Ethel Dyer, Bessie Harding, ?, Agnes Huish, Em Hawkins, Sally Rexworthy, Winnie Pollard, Annie Ridler, Annie Gooding, Annie Pulsford, Mary Webber, Ada Gooding, Alice Middleton, Mabel Hobbs, Mabel Yeandle, Maud Dyer, Ethel Ridler, Alice Ward; front: Charlie Bowen, ?, Herbert Rook, Cecil Rook, Martin Snell, Bill Pollard, Jim Pollard, Bob Rawle, Bill Bond, Bill Yeandle, Cecil Westcott, Charlie Harding, Fred Willicombe, Ernie Gooding, ? Bowen, Albert Bowen.

Chapter 7: Education

One of the earliest schools in Porlock is believed to have been held in the room over the church porch, which is now the Chapel of the High Cross. This room was probably the monks' room and, no doubt, was used by them to hold the vestments and other valuables of the Chantry. The room was neglected after the Reformation until the 18th century when the Church espoused the cause of educating the poor and it was once again used to teach local children to read and write.

Still visible are traces of an outside staircase which was erected to enable the children to attend school without going into the church (*see illustration on page*

The school yard, c.1910. (PM)

46). In a report to a House of Commons enquiry of 1818 Mr Passmore, the curate, said:

There is a small day school here, supported by voluntary subscriptions, consisting of 23 children. The poor are very anxious to have their children educated and would be thankful of any assistance offered them.

The Tithe Map of 1841 shows a school in the property of a Christopher Ridler, behind what is now Jana Henrie, the drapery shop, but in 1870 the Exeter District (Wesleyan) Education Committee reported: 'It is very desirable that there should be a day school at Porlock, the difficulty is the want of a suitable room'. Some 18 months passed before the Porlock Trustees decided to start day classes, probably in the little Sunday School room of the chapel and a schoolmistress was engaged from London. No records of the school have so far been found. *Morris's Directory of Somerset and Bristol* (1872) states: 'The Wesleyans have a place of worship here and there are day and Sunday schools for both sexes'.

The Porlock National School (C of E) for 150 children was opened in 1876 (which building now houses Porlock Information Centre, the library, the Lovelace Centre and the Parish Council Office). The following year in May the District Committee (Wesleyan) reported tersely: 'Porlock day school has been discontinued'. It is interesting that in a report of 1876 the admission registers of the New School show that pupils came from two sources, Porlock Old School and Porlock Weir Dame School. There is no mention of any pupils coming from the Wesleyan school, although the Wesleyan scholars were apparently transferred there almost immediately, together with their schoolmistress, Miss Woodger, who married Mr Elijah Stenner (senr). The new school was opened on Easter Tuesday 1876 and the children gathered at 9a.m., beginning work after a short service and an address from the rector. The fees were 2d. for the first child and a penny for each other member of the family. A night school was started on 2 October 1876.

There were school holidays for Whit Monday and Tuesday, for the Forester's Fête Day on 2 July, for Porlock Club Day on 6 July and for the Harvest Home on 12 September. The school did not close for Porlock Fair on 12 October, but there were several truants. In July 1877 the school closed early for the summer holidays because so many children were absent picking whortleberries (known locally as 'worts') and this adjustment to the timetable became a custom which lasted for many years.

In recent years Porlock has waited patiently for a new school which finally arrived after a site on the daffodil field between the Old Rectory and the Coach Road became available. The topping out ceremony was held on 22 February 1993 followed by a tea in the Old School Hall. The bell of Porlock Old School was moved to the new site, and the retired rector, Revd Cyril Munt, who had done so much to get the new building, came back for the ceremony.

The school was officially opened on 7 July 1993 by Lady Gass, Chairman of Exmoor National Park. Also present were Mrs S. Kevan, headteacher, the Bishop of Taunton, Rt Revd Richard Lewis, the rector of Porlock, Revd Barry Priory, the Methodist minister, Revd David Vale and Revd Parfitt, the Diocesan Education Officer. Since the closure of Allerford School (it is now the West Somerset Rural Life Museum), children also come from that village to attend school in Porlock and the pupils leave at the age of nine to be taken by bus to school in Minehead.

Porlock schoolchildren, 1926. Left to right, back row: Bob Williams, John Daish, Tom Sully, Reg Sage, Fred Stuckey, Herbie Court, Linda Bryant, Margaret Rogers; 3rd row: Brian Arnold, Ken Pollard, Ada Brooks, 'Birdie' Bushen, Nellie Mills, Lottie Chiswell, Una Blackmore, Freda Richards; 2nd row: 'Sonny' Grandfield, Charlie Hawkins, Douglas Rawle, Tom Down, Sid Bass, Noah 'Nobi' Pollard, Monica Ridler, Lily Westcott, ?, Lily Burgess, Gordon Reed; front: Sid Ward, Glyn Willicombe, Reg Webber, Owen Stenner, Arthur Pollard, John Norman, Betsy Hawkins, Anita Piper, Betty Daymond, Lily Bass, Patsy Rawle, Donald Grandfield, Ken Martin, Hilda Brown. (PM)

Porlock schoolchildren, c.1926-27. Left to right, back row: Joan Cape, Jack Rew, Joan Pugsley, Susie Pengelly, Jack Percival, Lily Palmer, Gwen Middleton, Ruth Pugsley, Jack Comer; 3rd row: Peggy Cooksley, Alfie Floyd, Jack Elsworthy, Florrie Rawle, Ena Bray, Winnie Hancock, Gwen Ferris, Nancy Cape, Edith Rew, Jean Rawles; 2nd row: Doreen Daymond, Francis Rawle, Doreen Ferris, Nelly Coles, Iris Bray, Mary Norman, George Bushen; front: Joyce Hensley, Basil Cooksley, Ivy Norman, Florrie Hancock, Fred Cape, Sam Rawle, Ethel Rew, Mary Pengelly, Rita Middleton, Arthur Palmer, Joyce Palmer, Joan Bushen. (PM)

Porlock School, 1900. The headmaster, Mr Brooks, is on the left. (PM)

Left: *The west end of the school with the railings on the left. The two cottages were knocked down to make the entrance for the High Bank Bungalows, the caravan park and the fire station. (PM)*

Right: *Here's discipline – all in step. Ridler's Boot and Shoe Shop is on the left of the picture, now the Real McCoy Saddlery. (PM)*

Porlock schoolchildren, 1971. Left to right, back row: Miss E. Organ, Lester Williams, Malcolm Prescott, Ivor Cooksley, Neil Palmer, Philip Purvis, Martin Sparks, Peter Doddimead, Miss Smith (student teacher);
3rd row: Karen Chilcott, Shirley Gibbons, Dawn Cooksley, Nicola Moles, Tracey Westcott, Katrina Floyd, Audrey Cameron, Pauline Doddimead, Annette Corner, Ann Leader;
2nd row: Dawn Cridland, Annette Bryant, Maureen Gibbons, Angela and Nichola Leach, Jaqueline Nancekivell, Gilian Brooks, Tina Moles, Anita Williams, Tracey Dascombe;
front: Vincent Court, John Purvis, Christopher Binding, Kevin Bridgewater.

Porlock schoolchildren, 1978. Left to right, back row: Simon Hogg, Michael Wilde, John Richards, Neil Binding, Simon Fry, Andrew Cridland, Grant Bloys;
4th row: Sarah Nancekivell, Lisa Bryant, Maxine Sudds, Emma Sully, E. Lushmore, Mandy Gibbons, Marie Purvis, Hannah Fry;
3rd row: Frazer Guiness, Matthew Hawkins, Nick Coward, Christopher Chiswell, Shane Prideaux, Seymour Hammett, Malcolm Corner, Matthew Griffiths, Barry Cooksley, Michael Keal, Paul Richards, Neil Williams;
2nd row: Charmain Tucker, Kate Lamacraft, Claire Johns, Lisa Morris, Emma Keeling, Victoria Hooper, Ann Richards, Erica Sully, Jacky Urry, Vanessa Shopland;
front: Leo ?, Derek Nation, Andrew Burge, Stephen Keal, Susannah Brown, ?, Theresa Bryant, Ann Price, Maria Adams, Amanda Nation, Julia Kisby.

St Dubricius First School, Porlock, 1992. Left to right, back row: Hazel Burge, Ross Sweetland, Scott Huish, Tim Biddiscombe,
Robin Tucker, Robert Southey, Peter Mounfield, James Owen, Ben Morris-Taylor, John Stapleton, Alex Leader;
5th row: Lucy Barney, Hayley Richards, Leanne Beart, Emma Lee Hulbert, Gillian Hampsey, Katherine Haw, Cara Dawid,
Charlotte Rich, Kelly Needs, Sam Selley, Samantha Westcott;
4th row: Hayley Oates, Molly Moloney, Joanne Needs, Susie Keal, Amy Westcott, William Thompson, Lucianne Bryant,
Kevin Sparks, Mark Wilson, David Mounfield, Laura Hoskens, Kirsty Binding, Molly Rooke, Adam Sparks, Tom Leader;
3rd row: Vicki Keal, Keith Needs, Greg Richards, Sarah Meecham, Orlando Brown, Dominic Westcott, Wayne Gummer,
Stephen Harding, James Burge, Dominic Healey, Katie Sadlier, Richard Meade, Matthew Morris, Adam Rowlinson, Rory Crabb;
2nd row: Anthony Norris, William Ellicott, Sarah Harding, Sam Taylor, Arnica Bickerstaff, Jenny Snell, Max Samuel,
Georgina Thompson, Robin Pilcher, Joel Dawid;
front: Abigail Moloney, Caroline Smith, Luke Cooksley, Laura Meecham, Duncan Westcott, Caroline Westcott, Helen Robinson,
Lewis Rich, Stephen Spurrier, Richard Binding;
staff: Sue Wyatt (left, back), Julie Biddiscombe (left, centre), Martina Keal (left, front), Sue Flatley (centre, left), Sue Kevan (centre),
Julia Holdback (centre, right), Jeanette Perkins (right, back), Hazel Oates (right, 3rd), Judith Wescott (right, 2nd),
Chris Moon (right, front).

THE BOOK OF PORLOCK

The old school shortly before it was closed. (GW)

The new school. (GW)

Chapter 8: Time and Tide Wait for No Man

Few places in the world seem to have escaped unwelcome visitations by extreme weather in some shape or another and natural disasters are reported so regularly as to seem almost a daily occurrence. In Britain, we are lucky enough to enjoy a relatively calm state of affairs by the standards of many other regions, but there are exceptions and Porlock has not been without its disasters and mishaps at the hands of fire and flood, winds and snow.

One of the earliest recorded events concerns one Grace Mogridge, a widow of Porlock whose house and grounds were lying near the sea by a small lake, 'whose discent is from a very steepe woodie mountayne'. It appears that her house, out-houses, fishing equipment, garden and two acres of hops, along with all other remaining possessions, were washed into the sea, to the total value of over £200. A petition signed by two magistrates and 27 residents of Porlock was made at quarter sessions at Wells on 11 July 1626 where it was decided to advance 'the poor woman £6.13s.4d. towards her relief in this her extremitie'.

In 1910 came the event which local folk have referred to for many years as the 'Tidal Wave' or 'Wash Out' at Porlock Weir. Many houses were flooded and the roads covered in pebbles and so high was the water that boats were rowed along the street at Porlock Weir.

Nor did the village escape entirely from the effects of the Lynmouth flood of 1952, but the torrential rains of 1960 brought more serious repercussions when, during a very heavy storm, the Hawkcombe stream became choked in several places and the roads in Hawkcombe and Sparkhayes were washed out leaving many shops and houses flooded up to a depth of 4 feet.

Hurricanes have also visited their force on the

The snow of 1978 blown up into fantastic shapes like icing on a cake and frozen solid. (DC)

parish over the years, destroying personal property and countless ancient trees in the surrounding woodlands. High tides whipped up by gales have repeatedly broken through the pebble ridge and flooded Porlock Marsh, resulting in the drowning of many sheep. With the constant erosion of the coast over thousands of years the area has changed dramatically. Following the breach of the pebble ridge on several occasions during the 1990s, no further work has been done, as it once was, to refill the gap. As a result, it has widened considerably and the shingle has moved further and further up the beach bringing about a total change to the Marsh, which has now become a salt environment. Much of the original flora has perished, as have the reed bed and willow trees, and new types of plants are colonising the area. Much of this is of concern to both locals and visitors who loved to walk in that area and, as the coast path has been breached, it can now be dangerous to try to cross that gap where the water flows in and out at a force capable of sweeping a person off their feet. At present approximately 60 per cent of tides now flow in and run up through the Marsh and several fields almost to Bossington's lime kiln.

That this has happened many times before during the last 8000 years is well evidenced and research suggests that changes will continue. There is a submerged forest in Porlock Bay and tree stumps are still visible at very low tides. Recently the remains of an aurochs, a species of huge wild cattle which roamed the land in ancient times, was discovered on the foreshore by the Countryside Manager of the National Trust. Radiocarbon dating has shown that the bones date from the early to mid Bronze Age and it is proposed that they be placed on permanent display in the parish.

FIRE

Left: *In 1928 Porlock witnessed a serious fire at the house known as 'England's' which had been used as a paint store for Charlie Nichols, a village painter. The Minehead brigade attended as Porlock did not then have its own and helpers passed up buckets to a nearby roof. (PM)*

Right: *Villagers thronged into the streets to help and watch. The chemist's and barber's shops can be seen on the right of the picture. (PM)*

Porlock Fire Brigade, c.1945. (PM)
Left to right: Jim Blackmore, Maurice Ladd, Jim Sparks, Charlie Sully, Albert Grandfield, Gordon Floyd, Sam Cooksley, Harold Rogers, Reg Squire, Jim Huish, Sid Squire, Ken Grandfield.

THE FLOODS OF 1960

Right: *This was the Doverhay at the end of the High Street during the floods of 1960. (VP)*

Below: *The flood water poured over the hedge at the junction of Sparkhayes Lane and Furzeland Road. (VP)*

Above left: *The land in Parson Street is flooded and the waters are so high that the footbridge seems in danger of being washed away. (VP)*

Above and left: *The damage to the road in Hawkcombe caused by the flood was extreme. In some parts it collapsed completely. (MI)*

Above: *The Marsh at a high tide seen from Porlock Toll Road and showing the gap in the beach. (MI)*

Left: *Very high tide in Sparkhayes Lane, c.1993. An RAF rescue helicopter, police and coastguard turned up when it was reported that someone was waving on the top of the beach. In fact it was just a floating tree with a branch swaying in the air! (DC)*

Right: *The tug* Triton, *which sank in the bay on 28 July 1938 when it was swamped by a barge in tow. The Lynmouth lifeboat was launched but all seven crew managed to swim ashore. The tug was drained and sealed at low tide the next day and refloated. The barge, meanwhile, was washed to near the top of the beach where the gap is today.*

Above: *The remains of Rockford Cottage, an old boat-house west of Porlock Weir and belonging to Ashley Combe. Repeated landslips along this coast will eventually destroy the cottage.*

SNOWBOUND IN PORLOCK

Left: *After the blizzard of 1978 in the Villes Lane footpath. (DC)*

Below: *The Toll Road completely blocked in 1963. The snow plough only clears Porlock Hill. (MI)*

Above: *In 1978 no cars were driven over this road, nor from Porlock to Minehead for five days. (DC)*

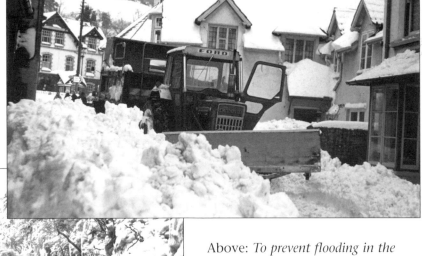

Above: *To prevent flooding in the case of a quick thaw, the snow was loaded onto a lorry and taken to Porlock Weir Car Park where it was then pushed into the sea, 1978. (MI)*

Left: *The road near Culbone Stables completely blocked in 1963. The road was impassable for several weeks. (MI)*

Stagecoach descending Porlock Hill, c.1915-20. Note the drag shoe under the rear wheel, attached to the coach by a chain and used to act as an extra brake. (PM)

Passengers arriving at Porlock's Ship Inn aboard the Lynton to Minehead stagecoach, c.1910. (PM)

Chapter 9: Travel and Transport

In ancient times, people moved about on foot or horseback using the old trackways, many of which favoured the high ground and can still be traced on Exmoor. Pack horses were used extensively for centuries and in coastal regions there was, of course, the sea.

A directory of 1794 states that 'There is no road West of Minehead suitable for carriages and therefore no mail, stage coach or wagon can get through', a report which is verified by the historian, Collinson, who, in 1791, writes: 'Most of the roads are so poor and the fields so steep that no carriage of any kind can be used... ', adding, '... all the crops are therefore carried in crooks on horses, and the manure in wooden pots call dossels'. Robert Southey, the poet who stayed at Porlock's Ship Inn in 1797, said: 'This place is called in the neighbourhood 'The end of the World', all beyond is inaccessible to carriage or even cart. A sort of sledge resting of two poles like cart shafts is used by country people'. Perhaps if there had been no easy access by sea there would have been a better road sooner but conditions were certainly slow in improving and in 1812 those of the road over Porlock Hill were so dire that the local inhabitants were presented at Quarter Sessions (*see overleaf*) for failing to keep it repaired.

The first stagecoach appeared in Porlock in 1843, the occasion being a special excursion to Lynton. Many of the villagers gathered to see this event and to read the decorative writing on the side of the coach. The railway reached Watchet 19 years later in 1862 and a party went from Porlock to see the first train arrive. The line was continued to Minehead in 1870 and plans to extend to Porlock and on to Lynmouth were submitted in 1898. However, there was so much local opposition that the scheme was never carried out.

Porlock Hill is said to be the steepest main A road in England and is known worldwide for its fierce and winding gradient. It was approached with much trepidation in the early days of motoring, as well as by the passengers on the stagecoaches. The distance from the Ship Inn to the AA box is approximately three miles, the steepest part between the first and the second bend is 1 in 4 or

Tourists brave the steep gradients of Porlock Hill in charabancs, c.1920.

25 per cent and the height at the AA box is a little over 1400 feet. Little wonder that two extra horses were needed to pull the stagecoach much of the way from the Ship Inn to the top. The stagecoaches used from Minehead to Lynton were mainly the 'Red Deer' and the 'Lorna Doone' and the service finally finished in the 1920s. The first car to climb Porlock Hill was driven by Mr S.F. Edge in 1900 for a wager and the first motorbike was driven up in 1909. The first car regularly used in Porlock was driven by Mr Frank Pocock for Mr Pearce, the tanner, before the First World War, and the first motor bus appeared in the same year. During the years after the First World War, when the bus was driving the stagecoach out of existence, the old and the new met face to face on the narrow road at Holnicote and for a while neither would give way to the other.

One of the most famous stories surrounding the hill concerns the transportation of the Lynmouth lifeboat over the moors and down to Porlock on 12 January 1899 in order to launch at the Weir and save a large sailing vessel, the 2052 ton *Forest Hall* (see Leisure and Rural Pursuits). A happier event, which came to the area once a year on Easter Saturday, was the exciting London to Lands End Motor Trials.

Motor coaches were run by various companies in Minehead taking visitors out on trips to see places of local interest. Football teams were taken with their supporters to away games and regular bus services were organised. In 1916 the Porlock Weir, Porlock and Minehead Motor Service Company Ltd. was established. It was started by local people and operated for over 40 years, running a daily service between Porlock Weir and Minehead. This company was known as the Blue Motors and others included Hardings, Staddons, Scarlet Pimpernel and Mascot, the latter being taken over by the Western National. The service between Porlock Weir and Porlock grew so popular that by the 1950s Blue Motors and Western National got together and, in the summertime, ran 18 journeys each way. On occasions it was necessary for the conductor to run to the telephone box and ring the depot at Minehead to send a duplicate bus!

William Vaughan Esquire Sheriff of the *County of Somerset*.
To the Inhabitants of the *Parish — of Porlock —*
— in the Hundred of *Carhampton*
in the County of *Somerset.*

BY VIRTUE of his Majesty's Writ, directed to the Sheriff of the County of *Somerset,* you are hereby summoned and required to be and appear before the Keepers of his Majesty's Peace, and his Majesty's Justices assigned to keep the Peace in and for the County aforesaid, at the next General Quarter Sessions of the Peace, to be holden at *the City of Wells* — in and for the said County, on Monday the *eleventh* — Day of *January* — next, then and there to answer our Sovereign Lord the King, touching and concerning certain Nuisances, Contempts, and Misdemeanors, in not repairing and amending a certain Part of the common and public Highway in the said *Parish* — (that is to say) *from the West end of the Town of Porlock towards and unto the Boundary of the parish of Culbone including the whole of Porlock Hill in length two Miles and a half and in breadth twelve feet*

whereof you stand *presented* — And hereof fail not at your Peril. Dated the *twenty eighth* Day of *October* — in the Year of our Lord, One Thousand Eight Hundred and *twelve*.

By the same Sheriff.

To the Bailiffs of the Hundred of *Carhampton* — —
——————— in the said County, and also to
James John Littley, and James Kingdon — and
to every of them to summon and warn. These.

Lewis, Printer, Wells.

EARLY MOTORING DAYS

Above: *Early motoring scene outside the Ship Inn showing what must have been one of Porlock's first traffic signs (on the left). (PM)*

Left: *An early motorcar, probably at the end of the First World War (as the Union flag and the French Tricolor are on show). The gentleman holding the child is the Revd Bunting, a former rector. Behind the driver is Mr Ernest Westcott. (PM)*

Ready to leave on an outing, early 1920s. (PM)

An outing to Windsor, c.1921. The passengers are riding in Hardy's coaches of Minehead. They must have continued their journey by train as the speed limit for such vehicles at the time was 12m.p.h. (PM)

Allerford (left) and Horner Water (right) pack-horse bridges in the neighbouring parishes of Selworthy and Luccombe.

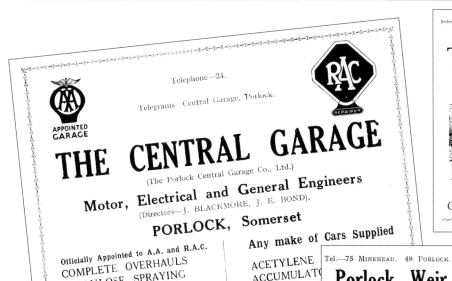

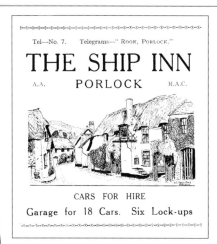

Advertisements for the Central Garage and the Porlock Weir, Porlock and Minehead Motor Service Company.
The detail from a 1935 poster for the Ship Inn gives an idea of how motoring tourists were bringing in business to the village.

MOTORING SPORT AND LEISURE

Above: *Mr Hawkins, who raked the road each week for the Council and made for a smoother ride up and down the hill (left). The road was not tarred until 1932. (PM)*

Right: *A motorcar passenger sitting on the back to put more weight on the driving wheels. The two girls in front are Winifred and Katie Burgess, c.1912. (DC)*

Left: *The London to Lands End Motor Trials were held each Easter, arriving in Porlock on the Saturday morning. This photograph is of the track on Doverhay Hill which no longer exists as it was washed out by the floods during the 1960s. (PM)*

MOTORING SPORT AND LEISURE

ROUNDING GREEN KNAP. PORLOCK HILL.

VOWLES. 4

Above: *A spill on Doverhay Hill, late 1920s. (PM)*

Left: *The trial on Porlock Hill, late 1920s. Every year hundreds of spectators flocked to the hill to witness this exciting event. (PM)*

*An overturned lorry on Porlock Hill, 1970s. The man in the white coat is Clifford
Charles, a reporter for the* West Somerset Free Press. *The AA man is Ted Lethaby with
Arthur Pollard on the right and Ted Forsyth on the left. (PM)*

*On 3 July 1996 at 7.35a.m. a horse box ran out of control on Porlock Hill and ran into the
garden of Woodfalls. Fortunately there were no horses in the box and only minor injuries were
sustained by the passenger. (DB)*
Inset: *Miss Violet Stenner looking at the damage after a runaway car on Porlock Hill crashed
into a window of Red Rose Cottage. (GH)*

An articulated lorry stuck on the second bend of Porlock Hill. An incident like this could close the road for several hours. (PW)

This articulated lorry blocked the road by the War Memorial for over four hours. It had passed the Horner turning, come down the old steep and tried to turn up the new steep – without success. It was finally freed by Ben Hammett who lifted the back around with the estate digger from Porlock Weir. (PW)

The Royal Oak and the Three Horse Shoes, c.1880. The Lorna Doone Hotel is now on the site of the latter. During the Napoleonic wars, the volunteers were trained by a sergeant major in the skittle alley at the back of the Royal Oak. (PM)

The old Castle Inn to the right of the cart looking east along the High Street, c.1870. The house behind is The Laurels, Porlock Abbeyfield. The houses facing the camera are at the bottom of Parson Street. (PM)

Chapter 10: Ale Houses and Inns

An ale house – sometimes called a 'tippling house' – was where beer and ale were brewed (and sold on the premises). Ale was the more ancient of the drinks, for beer, which included hops, was not introduced until 1400 from Flanders. In 1729 'Brewster Sessions' were instituted, at which retailers would be licensed by the JPs (Justices of the Peace). In a list for 1736 there were three people licensed to sell ale in Porlock: Nicholas Foy, John Stevens and Thomas Doyle, all of whom were vouched for by William Creech, who was probably the licensee of the Rose and Crown.

In 1740, ale house licences in Porlock were granted to Nicholas Fowey, John Stevens and Henry Randle. Here their proposer was Abraham Phelps.   John Stevens, who is mentioned in returns for 1736-61, is described as a 'victualler', and lived at Chantry Cottage, thought to have been an ale house at the time.

The list for 1744 gives eight names: Catherine Powell (Thomas Powell was at the Ship Inn, Porlock, from 1739-40, so she was probably his widow), John Stevens at Chantry, William Creech at the Rose and Crown, John Chibbett of Luccombe (probably Doverhay), John Franks of Porlock, John Shaplen, John Fowey and John Baker of Stoke Pero.

Ale house licences for 1746 were granted to: John Powell (Ship Inn, Porlock), William Creech (Rose and Crown), John Stevens (Chantry), John Chibbett, John Franks, John Stripling, John Fry and Elizabeth Jones. One John Thomas also wanted a licence for Horner Green.

Ale house licenses for 1756 were granted to: Joan Powell (a widow at the Ship Inn, Porlock), William Creech (Rose and Crown), John Stevens (Chantry), John Kent (White Horse), James Taylor (The Dragon), Thos Ford (Ship, Porlock Weir). In addition there were John Stripling, John Giles, John Gooding and Christian Gill (Cutcombe).

At a meeting of JPs in 1758 licences for innkeepers and 'victuallers' were applied for before a bench consisting of Sir George Trevelyan, Thomas Carew and the Revd Thomas Camplen. The meeting was held at the Three Cups Inn, Dunster, on 9 September 1758. The bench attended personally.

The 1761 licence read as follows:

These persons here-inafter named shall keep and maintain good order and rules and shall suffer no disorders or unlawful games to be used in the house or outhouse, yard, garden or back sides for the space of one year from the 29th day of this instant September – or there recongnizances to be void and a fine of £20 paid.

The old Rose and Crown Inn on the left which was closed down c.1870. The new Castle Hotel opened in 1900 and can be seen being built. The previous Castle Inn was sold in 1887. (PM)

PORLOCK INNS

	SHIP PORLOCK	CASTLE	ROSE & CROWN	THREE HORSE SHOES	ROYAL OAK	ANCHOR WEIR	SHIP WEIR
1794 Directory	George Ford		Sarah Rew				
1796 Land Ass.	George Ford		Mary Horn				
1805 Land Ass.	George Ford	OPENED ABOUT 1820	Mary Horn	Christopher Ridler		Henry Pulsford	Charity Poole
1822 Reg. of Inns	Nicholas Smith	Robert Falvey	William Jones	William Floyd		John Pulsford	Charity Poole
1830 Directory	Nicholas Smith	John Falvey	William Jones	David Knight		John Pulsford	Hugh Poole
1832 Electors	Nicholas Smith		William Bricknell	Christopher Ridler		John Pulsford	? John Perkins
1840 Tithe Map	Elizabeth Smith	George Stenner	William Bricknell	Edward Latham	Abraham Sparks	Ann Pulsford	Hugh Poole
1851 Electors			William Bricknell	John Fry			
1861 Directory	Elizabeth Smith	John Snow	Mrs Eliz. Stenner		Thomas Smith	William Pulsford	John Perkins
1870 Free Press			Summoned for rowdy behaviour	Mr G. Huish			
1872 Free Press	Mrs Pulsford		Mrs E.Stenner	Mr G. Huish			
		Sold 1887	CLOSED DOWN	Changed to LORNA DOONE			
1894 Directory	William Rook	James Perkins		Robert Stenner	Michael Ridler	J. P. Goddard	John Hobbs
1902 Directory	William Rook	Wheeler & Clatworthy		Walter Warman	Michael Ridler	J. P. Goddard	James Perkins

Lorna Doone Private Hotel
PORLOCK

Central
Position

———

Moderate
Terms

———

Modern
Conveniences

———

Proprietress :—

Miss
K. B. SMITH

———

Tel.:
Porlock 52.

Left: *The east end of the High Street showing the Lorna Doone Hotel, 1999. (PM)*
Right: *An advertisement for the hotel from the 1920s.*

Right: *Notice for the 1887 sale of the Castle Inn and various other lots in the parish of Porlock. The Castle was sold for £900.*

Below: *An advertisement for the Ship Inn, Porlock Weir, 1920s.*

PORLOCK & LUCCOMBE, SOMERSET.

Particulars of
FREEHOLD LANDS & BUILDING SITES,
THE CASTLE INN,
And other Business Premises and Private Dwellings,

◄ TO BE OFFERED FOR SALE BY AUCTION, AT THE SHIP INN, PORLOCK, ►

BY MESSRS.

HAWKES & RISDON,

TURDAY, 17th SEPTEMBER, 1887, at 2 p.m.

of Porlock Ford, will shew the Property, and further Particulars, with Conditions
of the Auctioneers, Williton, Somerset ; of

MESSRS. BAILEY, NORMAN, & BROWN,

Or of   8, Spring Gardens, S.W.;

MESSRS. WALTERS, DEVERELL, & Co.,

9, New Square, Lincoln's Inn.

Phone 25.
☩ The Ship Inn ☩
Fully Licensed
PORLOCK WEIR
An Old-World Hostelry with every modern convenience
a few yards from the Sea

LUNCHEONS :: TEAS :: DINNERS

Residential Terms on Application

THEN AND NOW

Left: *The stagecoach leaving the Ship Inn for Minehead, early 1900s. Some years before this picture was taken there was a sign (placed above the marker 'To Lynton') for the 'Exmoor Pharmacy' – Culverwell and Hawkins, Minehead. A cupboard for medicines was kept in the shop bearing the sign because there was no chemist in the village. (PM)*

Above right and right: *The Ship Inn in the late 1920s (drawing from an advertisement of the time) and in 1999. (PM) The establishment does not seem to have changed very much at all!*

The Castle Hotel, newly built in 1900 and (bottom) *in 1999. (PM)*

Above: 'Pudden' Floyd, a sketch by Francis Caruthers Gould. Pudden was a notorious character, featured in Exmoor Sporting and Otherwise. He was a keen hunting man and a poacher. Two Porlock men who were members of his 'gang' were caught in Hawkcombe at night by the police and gamekeepers, one with a gun, the other with the head of a stag. They were sentenced to a term of imprisonment for poaching but apparently Pudden always avoided being caught.

Opposite page: Lady Mary, Countess of Lovelace, laying the foundation stone of the Village Hall, 1925. The gentleman facing is John Cooksley, the local builder. The Porlock Girl Guides were in attendance. (PM)

Chapter 11: Prominent People

The Phelps family lived in Porlock from the 16th century and James Savage, in his book of 1830, *The History of the Hundred of Carhampton*, writes: 'A respectable family of the name of Phelps has long resided at Porlock, many of the individuals of which seem to possess an hereditary talent for drawing and painting!' Indeed, several churches in the neighbourhood have been ornamented by members of this talented clan – with coats of arms, commandments, texts, etc., and one of the family, Richard Phelps, studied painting under Thomas Hudson of Dunster and was a fellow pupil of Sir Joshua Reynolds. He completed many sketches and paintings, making copies of old masters and black chalk portraits, and, in his later years, often focussed on religious subjects. He painted for almost every family portrait gallery in the West of England, including those of the Aclands, Pophams, Carews and Bampfylds. He collaborated with Copplestone Ware Bampfyld of Hestercombe on a painting that includes life-sized self portraits of them both in 1785 outside the stable of Hestercombe House. This painting, which measures 12 by 13½ feet, was up for sale at a London Gallery for £25 000 in the late 20th century and unfortunately the Taunton Museum could not buy it. It is said that Richard Phelps also designed Conygar Tower at Dunster and even drew a design for a tower on Dunkery, which, fortunately, never materialised. The last member of the family to live in Porlock was Abraham Phelps who died in 1870.

Two other artists of note were father and son, both residents of Porlock and of the Gould family. The father, Sir Francis Carruthers Gould, built a house and retired to Porlock when he was still very active and commanded much respect in the later years of his life. He was a caricaturist for the *Pall Mall and Westminster Gazette* and from boyhood days in Barnstaple had two enduring interests – pets and politics – which absorbed him throughout his long and active life. Sir Francis produced a book of political caricatures and also one of caricatures drawn from nature, *Sketches from Exmoor*, which he did not, unfortunately, live to see published in 1929. His son, Alex Carruthers Gould, was an artist and worked from a studio in the Cleeve, Higher Doverhay. Many of his paintings – often landscapes of the Porlock area – can still be found in local homes.

Another artist who resided in Porlock was Fred Hall who had a studio here just after the turn of the century. Of the Newlyn School of artists, he

exhibited extensively both in Britain and on the continent and his work now fetches high prices. Leghe Suthers (1856-1924) was another 'artist in residence', also of the Newlyn colony. He painted extensively in the Porlock area where he had a studio, and where he died in 1924 at the Cleeve, Doverhay. He is buried in Porlock cemetery. Other artists who stayed and painted in the parish include Sir Alfred Munnings, Cecil Aldin and Lionel Edwards.

Porlock has also attracted many people with interests in horticulture and natural history, not least Norman Hadden, who lived at West Porlock and had a great knowledge of both plants and creatures, and developed lovely gardens. He began his woodland garden in Hawknest Wood in 1934 but this has sadly fallen into disarray. Several plants have been named after him, one being the Tree of Cornus 'Norman Hadden'. Together with E.W. Hendy, he produced a very comprehensive booklet entitled *A Guide to the Natural History of Porlock and District* (c.1930) which includes coverage of mammals, birds, reptiles, butterflies, moths, mollusca, wild flowers and fungi of the area. Mr Hendy himself was an eminent naturalist who specialised in wild birds. A Porlock resident, he lived in Bossington Lane where he built his house. He wrote several books, including *Somerset Birds and Some Other Folk* and *Wild Exmoor Through the Year*. It is interesting to note the changes that have taken place since the booklet was published – how many species were to be found in the Vale and which have now disappeared or become very scarce. The red squirrel, for example, was plentiful, especially in the Porlock Parks and there were no grey squirrels. Hares and water voles were quite common. and the red-backed shrike, or butcher bird, could be found in summertime, as could the nightingale. The corn crake was plentiful, the bittern could occasionally be heard on Porlock Marsh and black grouse were quite often seen on the surrounding moorlands. Yellow hammers and the cirl bunting were also seen regularly.

Two old Bossington characters enjoying their retirement, c.1950. On the left in the deckchair is Mr William Floyd who kept a caravan field and on the right is Mr William (Carrier) Floyd who followed his father as the local carrier from Minehead Station to the Porlock area. (PM, photograph by Percy Hitchcock FRPS)

Village chatter in Old Parson Street. The houses on the right were demolished to widen the road in c.1885 and the only house now recognisable is the old Rose and Crown in the centre at the furthest point in the picture. (PM)

Chapter 12: Memories of Village Life

During the 19th century the government of the village was in the hands of the Church and the Vestry was responsible for the upkeep of the roads and the assistance of the poor, as well as for the running of the Parish Church itself. These services were paid for by the Church rate, levied on every householder in the village. It was not until 1875 that the rate was abolished. In 1856 John Huish was paid £5 to collect the levies – at a rate of 5d. in the pound – and in 1858 William Fry and David Ridler were appointed overseers of the poor.

The Poor House was situated in the yard on the Porlock Weir road (where the Old School was built in 1875) and was closed when the workhouse or 'Williton Union' opened in 1838. The building could house 300 paupers who were all moved from poor houses across West Somerset. Hard working conditions in former times are well documented and the following is an excerpt from the apprenticeship agreement of a Porlock Weir man:

Training a Ships Carpenter 1866: Noah Henry Pollard puts himself apprentice to James Pollard of Porlock Weir for seven years. He is to be given subsistence but not paid until the third year, when he is to receive three shillings per week, rising to eight shillings in the seventh year.

Around this time, John Takle was paid £30 for keeping all of the parish roads in good repair. In 1869 the Vestry meeting adjourned to the Weir to view the road adjoining the sea and recommended that it be joined with the road from Porlock Ford making the present lower road to the Weir.

The first Parish Council election was held in 1894 and was an exciting occasion in the village where only rarely did something truly memorable happen. The following are a few memories and reminders of village life which have been recorded over the years.

In August 1878 the Prince of Wales, later King Edward VII, came to hunt on Exmoor. The hounds met at Hawkcombe Head and a crowd of 15 000 people was estimated to have followed – between 1200 and 1500 of those were mounted. The hunted stag was finally at bay in the Doone Valley and the huntsman, Arthur Heal, handed the Prince his hunting knife. The Prince delivered the 'coup de grace' with a swift stab to the heart and instant death to the stag. A disturbing rumour was abroad in the streets and clubs of London that evening – 'The Prince had committed suicide'! The London newspapers reported the event thus: 'The stag was killed in the Doone Valley, the Prince cut his throat'.

When the Royal Engineers were in Porlock, they had a lorry park in the orchard at Court Place Farm. The farmer had 20 ducks at the farm and one morning all the ducks had disappeared, the farmer called the police, and suspicion fell on some of the soldiers. The police visited the barracks at the Tannery and were shown around by the Company Clerk. They were particularly interested in seeing the kitchen and, looking into the cooking pot, they asked what was cooking. 'Beef' was the reply, and the police, being satisfied, left. All the time the Clerk was hoping that the police wouldn't notice the stag's head hung up on the wall. Someone had gone up on to the moor the previous night and shot a stag and the beef in the pot was really venison. The ducks meanwhile had apparently departed on the early morning train from Minehead to London where they were probably served up in a West-End restaurant the following night.

A scene that has been oft repeated by the locals and which also appears in *Exmoor Sporting and Otherwise*, occurred at Culbone Church one

Porlock. High St 1906.
Many thanks for the Devonshire Cream which arrived quite safely.
Trusting that you are well.

The Stenners outside Banksia House, Bossington. Left to right: Mr Elijah Stenner junr,
Mr Elijah Stenner senr with wife, Flora, and daughters, Ruth and Winifred. (GH)

Left: *An inglenook as found in many of the old cottages around Porlock.*
Right: *The old doorway of Chantry Cottage in the Drang. (PM)*

The house on the left is Frazers, an old property rebuilt in 1903. The wall on the left belongs to the orchard where the new chapel was built in 1927 and the building on the right is Whortleberry House. (PM)

The mill pond behind Abbeyfield which has now been drained and built on. (PM)

The end of the hunt at Doverhay Farm, c.1910. Many villagers followed the hunt and often the stag would be killed in the village. The man standing in the cart on the left is 'Pudden' Floyd. (PM)

A similar picture taken at the junction of the Lynmouth-Porlock Weir road at the west end of the village. The man with the long white whiskers is another well-known character, Robert Stenner, the landlord of the Lorna Doone. A local story tells of how one day somebody cut off one side of these whiskers when Robert was sleeping. (PM)

quiet Sunday during summer. That day the small congregation of locals also included two visitors who had walked from Porlock Weir and who, the weather being warm, were dressed in white. All was well until the rector gave out his text: 'Who are these arrayed in white robes, and whence come they?' He was an impressive preacher and kept on repeating his text, his eyes seeming to fix on the unfortunate visitors. At last the Parish Clerk could stand it no longer and answered back: 'I don't exactly know who they be, but I believe they're stoppin' at the Anchor!'

Another Porlock story tells of an old chap who dozed off in the old Chapel one evening and, waking suddenly, exclaimed in a loud voice: 'Lime and dung is the stuff for taties'!

At times of stress people will say and do funny things – old Billy who used to deliver coal with a horse and cart is a case in point. He was at the top of Hawkcombe one day, when suddenly the horse dropped dead. 'I'm damned', he said, 'I've never knowed 'en do that before'!

Not so long ago a man called to deliver a load of logs to a lady who had recently lost one of her sisters. The lady had gone to the village, so she had left a note on her back door: 'Please leave a load of logs at my sister's, not the one that's died'.

In the 1960s the then Methodist minister, Revd Glynn Lister, played football with the Porlock team. In one match the local team were being hard pressed, and the Revd got the ball only to be loudly instructed to 'Run like hell, Vicar!'

When the weather cock was removed from the church steeple for refurbishment a hole was discovered through the tail of the bird. Hearsay has it that the responsible party was one Fred French of West Porlock, an old soldier who, after the First World War, worked for Mr Cape, opposite the church. One day Fred stood in the yard with a rifle and boasted that he could hit the weather cock. Of course he was told to prove it, took one shot and hit the bird which spun around many times.

A well-known local character was short of money one evening, so went home to his wife and said: 'Mrs, can you let me have 1s.6d. 'cos there's a feller down the Oak selling bags of fertiliser, and they says 'tis rippin stuff for taters'. The lady duly gave her husband 1s.6d. and he then went off to the Oak and spent a very pleasant evening with his friends. One Sunday evening several weeks later he went with his wife to the allotment to see how things were coming along. Remembering how she had donated the 1s.6d., she said: 'By the way, was that fertiliser any good?'. 'Oh yes', he said, pointing to some potatoes nearly ready for digging, 'look at them'. Then he pointed to a row only a few inches high which had been planted a

The centre of Porlock at the end of the 20th century – this spot has always been known as the Bridge because the main stream from Hawkcombe passes under the street here. (DC)

few weeks later. 'Look at the difference with those that didn't get any!' 'Oh', exclaimed his wife, 'if I had known 'twas that good I would have given you three shillings'.

A certain old man used to go to church on a Sunday evening. Others always knew when he arrived because he had a habit of knocking out his pipe on the tomb in the porch before coming in to sit down. One Sunday evening he arrived as usual, knocked out his pipe and put it in his jacket pocket. All remained uneventful until the sermon, when there was a sudden scuffle and an exclamation of 'I'm damned!'. His pipe had caught his pocket on fire.

One of the most interesting things in a book such as this is the surnames. Charles Chadwyke Healey in his *History of Part of West Somerset* gives a list of some of the names of taxpayers. In the time of Henry VIII those listed as being in Porlock are: Kent, Riden, Spurriers, Stevens, Taylor and Webber. Bossington names include Burgess, Chibett and Huish and, at Yarnor, Elworthy, Nichols and White. In Elizabeth I's reign the names Phelps and Slowley appear at Porlock, Rawle at Luccombe, Yarnor and Porlock, and Creech and Kitnor at Bossington. Arnold, Hole and Snow are also listed. Poole appears in the listings for Bossington in the succeeding reign. In the time of Charles I we have Bushen and Fry and many of these names are still represented in the district today.

The names Sparke and Bromham date back to the early Edwards and although some of the older names have now disappeared from Porlock, they can still be traced via the local tombstones or the tombstone book (compiled and researched by the Porlock W.I.) in the museum and library.

HIGH STREET

Left: *Chimney Cottage (and the cottages on either side of it) were among the oldest buildings in the High Street. Beyond, on the right hand side of the street, are houses of the Victorian era and even further along, Abbeyfield House and Bridge House which date from Georgian times. (PM)*

Right: *The High Street with signs on display for the public telephone and Kodak film. (PM)*

HIGH STREET

The Doverhay end of the High Street, c.1910. The house on the left is Vine Tree, now the Londis Store. Just visible on the wall is the advertisement for Taylor's Horse Bus Service to Minehead. (PM)

The same view in 1999. (PM)

Porlock High Street at the top of Sparkhayes looking up to Parsons Hill, 1926. On the right of the picture is the Huish family's tobacconist shop (advertised right). (PM)

D. J. HUISH
TOBACCONIST & CONFECTIONER
Porlock
—:—
APARTMENTS.

Looking up to Parsons Hill where the T.V. relay mast is visible, 1999. (PM)

The old farmhouse, Higherbourne, in the High Street. The farmer in the doorway, Dick Ridler, was also a butcher and known as 'Butcher Dick'. He was said to be a poor butcher as he only butchered half a cow a week. The farm was sold in 1910 and then demolished. (PM)

One of the row of shop buildings which replaced the farmhouse, 1999. (PM)

PARSON STREET

Above: *Looking up old Parson Street, c.1880. The building on the right is Bridge House, the houses on the left surrounded the churchyard. The road was widened on the left after the houses were knocked down. (PM)*

Above: *Looking down Parson Street in the 1930s.*

Right: *Looking up Parson Street, 1999. (PM)*

Red Rose Cottage

Left: *Red Rose Cottage with Pollard's Garage showroom on the left and the garage itself beyond the cottage. The cottage was the home of Mr Frank Norman and his niece, Miss Violet Stenner* (see also page 72). *(DC)*

Above: *The cottage was demolished in c.1975 to widen the road and allow for the development of land behind the building. (DC)*

Right: *New houses now called Pollards Court have replaced both the showroom and the site of the cottage. (DC)*

West Porlock looking towards Porlock.
The cottage on the left was destroyed by fire in the early 1920s. (PM)

The same group of houses looking the other way, 1920s. (PM)

Chapter 13: West Porlock and Porlock Weir

West Porlock is a hamlet with around 20 houses as well as an hotel. Until the last century there was a farm at Dunns Court and, until around 1930, a leather craft shop. There were also two generations of blacksmiths until the Second World War and the old village 'lock-up' (where offenders were held overnight) still stands in what was their yard.

Today Porlock Weir is still much enjoyed by both local people and visitors, it being a peaceful, old fashioned and unspoilt place. Although the former trade has ceased and fishing has become almost a thing of the past, there is still a striking sense of tranquillity and beauty to be imbibed here.

During its transition from working harbour to tourist village, the people arrived by horse bus, and later charabancs and buses – there were few motorcars. Many spent their time swimming, fishing or taking trips with the local boatmen. The hotels and guest-houses were busy, as were the fishermen's wives who supplied trays of tea for visitors to take down onto the beach. The stables which once housed plenty of horses have now been converted into art and craft shops, and there is a black-smith, a glassblower and a clothing workshop. The Weir also boasts a boutique, a coffee shop and a village store.

Jack Moggridge, the last of the West-Porlock Blacksmiths. (PM)

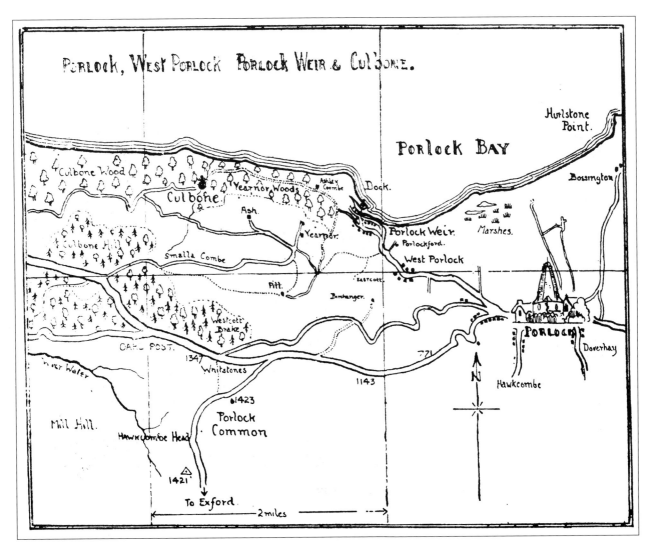

The Anchor Hotel at Porlock Weir before the new wing was built in 1902. The building on the right is now called Pieces of Eight but at this time was used as a flour store. (PM)

The Anchor horse bus with driver, Henry Pollard. (PM)

An early motoring scene at Porlock Weir, 1920s. (PM)

A postcard showing the inner harbour complete with footbridge, postmarked 1906.

Mr William (Fiddler) Pollard, an old fisherman who also dredged for oysters. (PM)

BILL POLLARD

HIS FACE IS KNOWN TO MILLIONS

By Daily Mail Reporter

A WEST - COUNTRY fisherman with a face known to millions, has died, 88 years old, at Porlock Weir, Somerset beauty spot.

Visitors to Porlock often turned to look at him as he hauled his boat up the beach.

His face, shadowed by an old trilby, seemed familiar—though they were sure they had not seen him before. Bill Pollard's photograph appeared throughout the country on advertisements of Capstan tobacco and cigarettes.

A director of the tobacco company, holidaying at Porlock several years ago, was struck by his appearance. Bill agreed to be photographed and went back to his fishing.

Soon his picture had made him familiar to millions of smokers.

This old Somerset character used to boast that he could build, rig, and sail a boat. He was a pioneer of the oyster-dredging industry once carried on in Porlock Bay.

Oyster Perch

The workmen who worked on the restoration of the harbour in 1913 and photographed when the new lock gates were hung.
Left to right, back row: Ted Huish, Wilf Hobbs, Dick Hobbs, Tommy Hawkins, Jack Farmer, George Bushen, Albert Cooksley, Jim Bass,
Alf Slade, William Hawkins, ? Pugsley;
front: Walter Huish, Fred Huish, Dick Ridler, William Huish, James Huish, Dick Huish, Robert Huish, Nicholas Huish,
George Cooksley. (PM)

An early photograph of the Harbour Stores. The sign over the door reads 'Manley, Grocer'. Later it was H. Manley, followed by his son, Victor. The property on the right was a flour and grain store and is now a dress shop and café. (PM)

Gibraltar Cottages were built right on the edge of the beach. Beach Cottage is behind on the left and Lane Head Cottages, originally fishermen's cottages, are above to the right of the picture. (DC)

Lane Head Cottages. (DC)

An old photograph looking across what is now the car park towards the Reading Room (now a cottage). (PM)

A busy day on the car park. The shipping trade may have declined but the visitors still enjoy Porlock Weir. (PM)

A photograph of 1908 on the lower road (made in 1894) to the Weir. Note the number of groynes on the beach. The long building on the left was the saltern where herrings were salted into barrels.

The top of West Porlock Steep. Little has changed since this photograph of c.1900 although the letter box in the wall is no longer there. (PM)

Right: *The ketch* Irene *in the dock for the filming of the* Feast of July *by H.E. Bates. This was the last vessel built and launched at Bridgwater (in 1907). Originally she traded to the continent and later in the brick trade to Liverpool and Ireland. She has been privately owned since 1965 by Dr L. Morrish and is used for charter work. (DC)*

Left: *An old ketch rotting in the inner harbour at the Weir. (PM)*

Below: *Left to right: Sid Stenner (harbourmaster), Arthur Ley, Captain Coates of the ketch* Democrat *and Preston Ley senr, 1954. (PM)*

A receipt of 1895 made out to William Pollard from Mr John Red for wares brought into the Weir on a ketch. (PM)

Left: *A summer scene, c.1950. The fishing boats also made trips around the bay during the holiday season and the little hut over the wall was used as a tea room for visitors. (PM)*

Right: *High tide on a tranquil day in the harbour. (PM)*

Below: *Porlock Weir harbour in the 1940s or '50s. The sluice house on the dock has been turned into a wartime pill-box. (PM)*

The inner harbour. Sailing ketches such as the one at the quay continued to bring in coal until 1950. (PM)

An old postcard of the inner harbour, c.1900. (PM)

Bristol Channel pilot cutters approaching the harbour, July 1998. At the turn of the century over 200 of these fine craft operated from the ports of Bristol, Newport, Cardiff, Barry and Swansea. They were used to put a pilot onto the large ships entering the Channel. Noted for their speed and excellent handling, they are now a rarity and the few that remain have been converted into pleasure craft. (DC)

The paddlesteamer Waverley *in Porlock Bay in 1996. Passengers are being landed and picked up by small boats – the first time this had happened for 60 years. (DC)*

Mr Preston Ley senr preparing his lines for fishing. (PM)

Chapter 14: Bossington

Bossington was at one time part of Porlock parish and dates back at least to Saxon times. In AD873 the name was spelt 'Bossingtune' which means 'the Tun of Bosa's people'. From AD920 it belonged to the Abbot of Athelney and at the Norman Conquest was given to Ralph de Limesi. The manor remained in the possession of the Abbey until the Dissolution of the Monasteries, since which time it has belonged to various families, including the Sydenhams, the Blackfords, the Dykes and the Aclands. In 1944 Sir Richard Acland handed the manor over to the National Trust, to which most of the properties now belong.

Bossington is something of a mecca for visitors, being very picturesque. The cottages and farm are of great age and built mainly of local stone, although many of the thatched roofs have been replaced by tiles. Bossington was once well known for its splendid walnut trees, the timber from which was valuable for both furniture and for musket stocks.

In *An Exploration of Exmoor* published in 1900, the author, John Lloyd Warden Page, describes the village:

Bossington is famous for its walnut trees, the largest an enormous specimen, sixteen feet in girth, and with branches in themselves as large as many a full grown woodland monarch.

The villagers were intensely proud of this, their only 'lion', and it was amusing to note the derision with which an ancient dame heard the suggestion that it must be a mere 200 or 300 years old. 'Lor' bless 'ee!', she exclaimed scornfully; 'he must be more than that; folks do come from all over the country to see 'un'.

After a complaint was made by Selworthy Parish Council regarding the danger posed by this monster, the tree was cut down in the first week of January 1952. From Bossington, it was taken to France to be made into veneers for furniture. Nobody was able to put a precise age on it.

Looking down from above Birchanger Farm to the Marsh at high tide. (DC)

A PICTURE POSTCARD VILLAGE

Right: *Bossington, c.1900. (PM)*

Below: *A 1920s advertisement for accommodation at Orchard House.*

ORCHARD HOUSE

BOSSINGTON, Allerford, Somerset

BOARD RESIDENCE.

Bath (h. & c.) Near Sea, Woodlands, and Moors.

TEA GARDENS.

Parties catered for. Terms moderate.
B. & B. 'Phone, 36 Porloc[k]

Below: *The higher end of Bossington village from a postcard of 1912. (PM)*

Above: *The ancient walnut tree at Bossington. (PM)*

The Higher End.

BOSSINGTON BEACH

Below: *When, on occasions of heavy rain, the pond burst through to the sea, the older people used to say 'The Devil's gone to sea'. The building on Hurlestone Point is the old coast-guard lookout built in 1902 and now disused. (DC)*

Above: *The Horner Water ends in a large pond at Bossington. (DC)*

Below: *Bossington Beach attracts many anglers. Photographed c.1965. (DC)*

BOSSINGTON BUILDINGS

Much of the thatch was replaced by slate during the 1800s. (DC)

Kitnors at Bossington showing the old-fashioned oven protruding from the chimney, 1995. (DC)

BOSSINGTON BUILDINGS

Top: *Beach stones were used in many Bossington buildings and walls. (DC)*

Above: *Bossington Chapel built in 1895, before which time services were held in various cottages in the village. (DC)*

Right: *The tall chimneys which characterise many of the houses in the village gave more draw to the fire, thus keeping the rooms free of smoke. (DC)*

View from Bossington Hill showing Porlock and Bossington, Horner Woods on the left and Hawkcombe Woods in the centre. (DC)

Workmen at Bossington, c.1880. All of these men would have worked on local farms or smallholdings although today few locals work on the land. (PM)

Porlock Home Guard at Court Place, 1944.
Left to right, back row: ?, Bill Keal, Raymond Keal, Stan Hooper, ?, Bill Thomas, Bill Thomas senr,
Bill Tame, Jeff Farrant, Tom Harris;
4th row: Revd J.A. Smart, Jack Mead, George Hill, Cecil Westcott, Bill Chiswell, Patrick Joyce,
Bert Tancock, Harry Rawle, Reg Huntley, Charlie Brooks;
3rd row: Tom Sully, Bert Gibbons, Alf Keal, Sid Rawle, George Bushen, Vivian Langrish,
Francis White, Clifford Barwick, Hertbert Kingdon, Henri Webb;
2nd row: ?, Arthur Ward, Jack Farmer, Ernest Sully, Fred Kent, Dudley Richards, Peter Leach,
Sid Gibbons, Fred Middleton;
front row (sergeants): Jim Wilson, Sid Ferris, Bill Yeandle, Sidney Bass, Bill Glasso, Fred Willicombe;
in front (officers): Captain Bill Parsons, Major Sandford, Lieutenant Hugh Webber.

Chapter 15: Porlock in Wartime

Porlock VAD (Voluntary Aid Detachment), 1914. Many of these ladies helped nurse the wounded soldiers at Minehead Hospital during the First World War. Left to right, back row: ?, ?, ?, ?, ?, Mrs Bill Pugsley, Mrs Selby, Miss B. John, Mrs Comer, Mrs Snell, Nurse Horden, Miss Luxton, Mrs Priscott (Luccombe), Miss D. Perkins (Ship, Porlock Weir); centre: Mrs C. Arnold, Miss Clark, Miss Orchard, Mrs Smart, Miss Peck (Commandant), Miss Fyffe, Mrs Clark, Mrs S. Arnold (Governess), Mrs Awdry, ?; front: Mrs Priscott (Luccombe), ?, ?, ?, Miss F. Burgess, ?, Mrs Comer, Mrs Rook. (DC)

Red Cross cooks at the VAD camp, c.1914. Centre left is Ernest Rew and centre right is Cecil Rawle. (PM)

WEST SOMERSET YEOMANRY

The West Somerset Yeomanry returning to their camp. The camps were held annually all over Devon and Somerset for the training of West-Country volunteers. (PM)

West Somerset Yeomanry Camp, June 1914. (PM)

WEST SOMERSET YEOMANRY

Marching behind the band back to the camp field. (PM)

*The Yeomanry attending service at the Band of Hope field on the
Minehead road. (PM)*

WAR MEMORIAL

Left: *General Peck unveiled the war memorial in 1921.*

THE MEN OF PORLOCK AND NEIGHBOURHOOD WHO GAVE THEIR LIVES FOR KING AND COUNTRY DURING THE GREAT WAR

Baker, R. Pte Som. LI
Beaumont, Checkland, M.B. Lieut W. Som. Yeomanry attd Som. LI
Binding, E.J. Pte Som. LI
Blackmore, J. Pte Som. LI
Bowden, H. Pte Oxf. & Bucks. LI
Coles, G.H. Corpl Som. LI
Hensley, R. Pte Som. LI
Hobbs, F. Driver RASC
Hobbs, H.A. Pte Som. LI
Huish, A.J. Pte D. of Corn. LI
Huish, C.G. Pte Devon Regt.
John, W.F. CYS *HMS Lion*
Moore, W. Pte Welch Regt.
Pollard, N. Pte Som. LI
Pugsley, E. Sapper RE
Ridler, H.W. Gunner RGA
Riley, J. Corpl D. of Corn. LI
Rogers, J. Pte KOYLI
Squire, S. Pte Som. LI
Stenner, B. Pte RASC MT
Stuckey, G.E. Pte Som. LI
Sully, R. Pte Lond. Regt.
Titley, A.G. Lieut, W. York. Regt.
Ward, A. Pte Som. LI

The Unveiling

OF THE

Porlock and Doverhay War Memorial.

SUNDAY, JULY 24TH, 1921,

At 3 p.m.

Order of Service.

HYMN.

O GOD, our help in ages past,
Our hope for years to come,
Our shelter from the stormy blast,
And our eternal home;

Beneath the shadow of Thy Throne
Thy saints have dwelt secure;
Sufficient is Thine arm alone,
And our defence is sure.

Before the hills in order stood,
Or earth received her frame,
From everlasting Thou art God,
To endless years the same.

A thousand ages in Thy sight
Are like an evening gone,
Short as the watch that ends the night
Before the rising sun.

Time, like an ever-rolling stream,
Bears all its sons away;
They fly forgotten, as a dream
Dies at the opening day.

O God, our help in ages past,
Our hope for years to come,
Be Thou our guard while troubles last
And our eternal home. Amen.

SECOND WORLD WAR

War was declared on Germany on 3 September 1939, the first evacuees – schoolchildren with their teachers – having arrived two days earlier. The London children settled quickly into country life and ways and were soon learning the local dialect and, of course, the village children also picked up the London speech and sayings. Mothers with babies soon followed and, after Bristol was bombed, more evacuees arrived.

Rolls of barbed wire covered the length of the beach where pill-boxes were also erected; two remain at Porlock Weir, three at Bossington and one at West Porlock. German planes passed over on bombing missions, especially when Swansea was bombed and the fires could be seen from the Weir road. Convoys of ships were also often to be spotted out at sea but, apart from such sitings, Porlock did not suffer a great deal from the effects of the war. Several aircraft made forced landings or crashed in the Vale; those resulting in loss of life being the 'Halifax' at Ashley Combe, and the American bomber, the 'Liberator', which crashed on the Marsh on 29 October, 1942. The crew are honoured with a small memorial which stands there (*above*). A German Junkers 88 was also shot down on the beach (and the rear gunner killed).

The most notable event occurred in 1940, when, on 16 January, at the time of the great frost when the roads were covered in ice, an oil tanker was seen to be on fire west of Porlock Weir. Flames

rose several hundred feet, and the smoke several thousand feet into the air. Nothing could be done to save the ship or the 45-strong crew who were all lost. We now know that this ship, the *Inverdargle*, built in 1938, was sailing from Trinidad to Avonmouth and carried 12 554 tons of aviation spirit when she was torpedoed by a U-boat (*U33* under the command of K.L.Wilhelm V. Dreski).

The Army moved into Porlock in 1940 after the evacuation at Dunkirk. First came the 58 company of Royal Engineers, who were later replaced by 65 and 88 companies who specialised in chemical warfare. Thousands of troops came to Exmoor on manoeuvres and a tank-firing range was set up on North Hill in Minehead. Naturally, civilians were excluded from these areas. The British Army was followed in Porlock by the American Army, who trained on Exmoor, and the Tannery served as the barracks for both British and US soldiers alike.

The local Home Guard was training regularly, and the girls of the Timber Corps worked together with the men in the local woods felling trees.

Porlock fared better than many other places during the war, the only real interruption being the activities of troops in training, and villagers were not subjected to air raids. However, several Porlock men were prisoners of war and 13 men from the village gave their lives. Their names now appear on the war memorial, and a little garden of remembrance planted with 13 trees is sited at the bottom of the recreation ground.

HMS Porlock Bay, *a frigate built and launched in Bristol in 1945. She visited Porlock in 1946 when her crew were entertained by the residents. She then served in the America and West Indies Squadron. She was kept in reserve on her return to the UK before being sold to Finland in 1962 where she was renamed* Matti Kurki *and served as a training ship. She was finally sold for scrap in 1975.*

The original Porlock Band established in 1875. (PM)

Chapter 16: Leisure and Rural Pursuits

In the late 1700s the people of Porlock, as with many other villages, decided to form a Village Club. These clubs or 'Friendly Societies' were organised by the inhabitants with the aim of helping one another in times of sickness and distress – with the cost of funerals, for instance. Some of the money was spent on a day of celebration and in Porlock Club Day was a great event.

There were two clubs the village: the old club dating back to 1776, and the new club which began in 1819. The *Free Press* account of the anniversary of 1868 reads:

The clubs celebrated their anniversary on July 3rd. They assembled at their respective Inns; the old club at 'The Ship', and the new club at the 'Three Horse Shoes'. First to the Church for a service and a sermon by the Curate. Afterwards the band played on the Rectory lawn, then they went in procession to Court Place, before returning to their respective Inns for dinner. The rest of the day was spent in the customary way of these days, and all passed off with the greatest harmony.

Herbert Rook off to do some rabbiting. (PM)

The clubs disappeared in the 1880s, partly due to the competition of the Foresters, which began in 1875, and the Temperance Movement (1873), and partly because of widening interests and activities in the village community. The Henry Rogers Charity is still in existence, together with the Winsford Land Charity, both of which were founded by Henry Rogers, Lord of the Manor in the 17th century. These are some of the statements from new applicants to the Henry Rogers Charity as recorded in that organisation's book of 7 January 1843:

Elizabeth Marly of Porlock Weir, a widow of 85 years without any independent means of support. James Webber of Porlock Town aged 65, an old soldier, who was in the battle of Waterloo and twenty others in the Peninsular War. Now incapable of much. Henry Ellis, living in the Parson's Manor, aged 58, certified with his wife by Mr North. Is so afflicted, as to be unable to do much, having served one master 38 years. Lastly Philip Jones, aged 65 of Parsons Street, utterly debilitated by rheumatism, gout and asthma.

The Cricket Club was started in 1865 and the team played on the land known as the cricket field, later to become the recreation ground (which was opened in 1877). Rugby football was started in 1882 and the village switched to soccer in 1887. In 1883 the *Free Press* reported that:

Porlock seems to be partially undergoing a social revolution of late. The Blue Ribbon Mission has enrolled over 300 members under the temperance banner. The old Village Club being unable to walk this year, their festival day is going to be kept up by the Temperance party.

Other activities had also begun to be organised, including the setting up of a lending library which in 1889 had 200 volumes. There were also no less than three reading rooms – one in Dovery Manor, which is still there, one in Parson Street and also one at Porlock Weir which opened after the closure of the club on the harbour. Later a Band of Hope was formed and a report of 1907 tells us that a Temperance Tea was held at the Victoria Room, followed by games on the Rectory lawn. The Band of Hope also held an annual sports day in Powells field situated on the Minehead road.

Dances were held in the village school, as well as plays, comic operettas and music evenings. Every Whit Monday an afternoon fête was held in the recreation ground where there were stalls and sports of all kinds. Later in the year came the carnival. In more recent years Porlock has had many youth clubs, including packs of Scouts and Cubs, Guides and Brownies, and the Junior Red Cross. Porlock has been and still is a very active community.

THE PORLOCK BAND

Porlock people have always been very musical, with choirs, a choral society, and, on the lighter side, numerous variety concerts and operettas. Older Porlock residents will also remember the days when Porlock had a wonderful village band, which played together for many years. The last of the bandmasters was Harry Arscott who came from a highly musical family, several of whom played in the band. The first Porlock Band was started in 1875 with eight members: George Hawkins (Bandmaster), F. Hawkins, James Arnold, Philip Arnold, T. Radford, G. Norman and Noah Pollard.

Right: *Rules drawn up by the bandmaster included the following:*

* All members must conduct themselves to all engagements in an orderly manner and attend their duty.
* If absent, they must attend to their duty at the first cornet-call. If out of hearing without leave, they shall forfeit one penny.
* If any member at their meeting or engagements are found intoxicated or disorderly he shall forfeit 5 shillings. If the same offence be repeated, he shall be excluded.

THE PORLOCK BAND

Members of the band at practice, c.1920. Left to right, back row: Jim Cooksley, Ralph Radford, Charlie Arnold, Ernest Ridler, Jim Norman, Albert Burgess, Dave Dyer, John Norman; front: Reg Brown, ?, Ted Norman, Bob Moore. (PM)

Porlock Band at the Coronation celebrations, 1953. Left to right, back row: Gordon Delbridge, Dawn Perkins, Raymond Delbridge, Tommy Norman, George Williams, Tim Webber, Ewart Perkins, Bill Yeandle, Bill Williams; front: Bernard Arscott, Raymond Arscott, Hedley Pocock, Trevor Perkins, Robin Pugsley, Albert Slader, John Sparks, Reg Sage, Raymond Perkins, Gilbert Bellringer, Leslie Arscott, Charlie Arscott, Harry Arscott (Bandmaster). (PM)

ON A MUSICAL NOTE

Left: *Porlock Dance Band, 'The Merry Makers', c.1948. Left to right: Brian Middleton (accordion), Francis Lethaby (drums), Brian Richards (accordion), George Clements (trumpet), Rosemary Cape (née Gibbons, piano). (FC)*

Below: *Carolers from both churches during late night shopping, 1992.*

TocH Christmas party at Porlock Café, 1953. (Photograph by T. Blackmore, Minehead)
Left to right, back row: Bill Cook, Bill Collins, George Hall, Tom Norman, Bert Huish;
centre: Revd Ebeneezer Scott, Alf Cook, Ernie Pollard, Harry Crane, Dennis Corner,
Clifford Glanville;
front: Alf Floyd senr, Fred Scott (Minehead), Bill Williams, Revd Phillip Hughes,
Elden Arnold. (PM)

After being killed in the village, as was the custom at the end of many a stag hunt,
the animal was taken on a wheelbarrow to the butcher, c.1920. (PM)

*Members of the Ancient Order of Foresters on Walk Day, c.1910 in
Parson Street. (PM)*

*St Dubricius Church Handbell Ringers at a local gymkhana, 1930s.
Left to right: Reg Sage, Jim Huish, ?, Jack Forster, Jim Blackmore, Ron Blackmore,
Bill Huish, Sidney Daymond, ?. Conductor: Tom Cooksley. (PM)*

This photo is thought to be of a wedding celebration at the Lorna Doone Hotel, c.1910. The young man on the left is Edwin Smith who took over the saddlery business from his father. The shop is now a restaurant called 'Piggy in the Middle'. (PM)

Start of the marathon race, c.1909. (PM)

Porlock Football Team, 1899 season.

*Left to right, back row: Mr A. Floyd, J. Cooksley, T. Reed, S. Cooksley (Captain), W. Bromham, T. Westcott, P. Burgess, Mr L. Davies;
front: H. Perkins, F. Hooper, J. Hawkins (Vice Captain), W. Pugsley, J. Perkins. (PM)*

Charity finalists, West Somerset Cup, 1908.
Left to right, back row: Harry Perkins, Walter Chibbett, Bob Pugsley;
centre: John Perkins, Jack Roberts, Tom Westcott, Ernest Pugsley, Ernest Westcott,
Revd J.A. Smart, W. Petherbridge;
front: Harry Rawle, George Rawle, Dick Moore, Bill Pugsley, Gilbert Ridler. (PM)

Porlock Football Team with committee, 1920/21.
Left to right, back row: Harry Perkins, Ephraim Daymond, Tom Westcott,
Edwin Smith, ?, Bob Rawle, Jim Sparks senr, Cecil Ireland, John Perkins;
centre: ?, Ewart Perkins, Sid Bass senr;
front: Arthur Smith, Lionel Perkins, Clifford Burgess, Sidney Smith, Ted Huish. (PM)

Porlock Football Team, winners of the West Somerset League Shield, c.1960.
Left to right, back row: Cyril Baber, Jack Tucker, Fred Stuckey, Bert Maskell, Tom Moore;
centre: Arthur Ward (Linesman), Adrian Bryant, Tom Down, Ron Storey, Dan Maskell, Sam Rawle,
Owen Stenner, John Bracey, Tom Smith, Tony Dascombe, Fred Kent;
front: David Stuckey, Gerald Yeandle, Fred Cape, Derek Dascombe, Gordon Bellringer. (FC)

The team in 1974/5.
Left to right, back row: A. Ward, L. Bracey, D. Chilcott, S. Sully, G. Sizer, M. Graddon,
T. Webber, F. Cape;
front: J. Pollard, A. Heywood, P. Rawle, M. Plenty, K. Storey, G. Williams, D. Sheppard. (FC)

BILLIARDS AND CRICKET

Above: *Porlock Billiards Team, Doverhay Reading Room, 1960.*
Left to right, standing: Ron Blackmore, Bill Huish; seated: Ephraim Daymond, Jack Forster, Bill Piper. (PM)

Left: *Porlock Cricket Team, c.1960.*
Left to right, back row: Mrs G. Dascombe (Secretary), D. Dascombe, F. Cape, T. Smith, R. Squire, A. Bryant; front: W. Brown, V. Perkins, J. Bracey, M. Cooksley, K. Grandfield. (FC)

RECREATION AND SPORTING GROUNDS

Below: *Moving the old pavilion to make way for the new, c.1977*

Bottom: *Opening of the new tennis courts in 1971 by Miss Christine Trueman, former Wimbledon tennis star. To celebrate the opening she played the first match on the site against Miss M. Merson. Left to right: ? Stevens, C. Glanville, N.V. Meacham, W.R. Hadley, P. Sizer, Miss Trueman, J. Lynn, Miss Merson, C.W. Ireland, T. Sparks, L. Jones, Mrs M. Brown.*

Above: *The re-opening of the children's playground in the recreation ground, 1978 - all eager to get in! (PM)*

RECREATION AND SPORTING GROUNDS

Above: *Opening of the Recreation Ground Pavilion, 1978. Left to right, back row: W.R. Hadley, ?, M. McCoy, J. Lynn, P. Sizer, C. Bodman, N.V. Meacham, R. Binding; front: M. Keeling, O. Reeves, J. Sparks, M. Brown, A. Allen, S. Binding, E. Stevenson, D. Green, P. Bodman.*

Right: *A game of bowls in progress on the green.*

A day of celebration for St Dubricius Church Sunday School. Stenner's Bakery is on the right, Burgess' is on the left behind the banner. The band is probably the Band of the Somerset Light Infantry. (PM)

An old folks party outside the Old School in Parson Street, c.1870. The old man on the right with a walking stick is apparently suffering from bad rheumatism. The gentleman in the top hat and gaiters is perhaps the bishop. (PM)

A TocH party for the older folk of Porlock and Selworthy parishes, c.1970. An annual tea followed by a concert was given for all pensioners by TocH over a period of 33 years. For many this was a rare opportunity to meet together. (DC)

Porlock Weir Scouts (to the far left of the picture) on St George's Day Parade at Dunster, 1935, with leader, Mr Harry Filtness. Left to right: Bill Ridler, Ernie Pugsley, Dick Ridler, Stephen Baldwin, Ivor Glanville. It is surprising that there were enough children at Porlock Weir to run both Boy Scouts and Wolf Cubs during the 1920s and '30s.

Porlock Scouts at Porlock Weir, 1944. (DC)
Left to right, back row: Donald Ferris, Dennis Corner, Bill Pugsley, Mrs Doreen O'Kell;
centre: Brian Middleton, Francis Lethaby, Gilbert Tancock, Michael Ireland, Robin Grant, John Smith, Ronnie Allen;
front: Geoffrey Perkins, David Salter, Tony Dascombe, Alan Perkins.

Scouts visiting Trafalgar Square from camp at Gilwell Park H.Q. camp site,
Chingford, Essex, 1950. (DC)
Left to right, back row: Adrian Bryant, Peter Rice, Dennis Corner, Bill Williams,
Leslie Ridler, Derek Dascombe, Raymond Ley, Alfie Keal;
front: Raymond Perkins, George Williams, Nigel Grandfield.

Porlock Scouts, 1981. (DC)
Left to right, back row: leaders, D. Corner (GSL) and B. Palmer (ASL);
3rd row, standing: Andrew Floyd, Simon Fry, Justin Sully, Grant Bloys,
Shaun Pearson, Malcolm Corner, Alex Tremaine, Jason Willicombe,
Nicholas Hawkins;
2nd row, seated: Damon Willicombe, Darren Ley, Simon Hogg, Andrew Cridland;
front: Matthew Hills (far left), Neil Binding, Simon David, Michael Keal,
Scott Prideaux.

CORONATION DAY, 1953

Coronation Fête. Left: Geoffrey Perkins who read the proclamation.
Right: Frank Cooksley, town crier for the day. (PM)

Peter Gibbons throwing balls at the coconut shy. (PM)

PORLOCK DRAMA

A scene from Devilry with the Doones, *a local scout and guide show in the Village Hall, January 1953. Left to right: Lorna Scudimore, Grace Yeandle, Virginia Gould, Janet Blackmore, Maureen Floyd, John Perkins, Julie Braund, ?, ?, ?, Penny Gould. (Photograph Porlock Scouts)*

Porlock Women's Institute play at the Regal Theatre, Minehead, c.1932. Left to right: Mrs T. Norman, Mrs H. Long, Mrs J. Floyd, Mrs A. Sedgebeer, Mrs K. Peel, Mrs J. Forster, Mrs C. Clothier, Miss D. Stenner, Mrs M. Squire, Miss N. Cape, Miss K. Burgess, Mrs E. Huish. Boys: Trevor Perkins, Leonard Hall. (PM)

STREET CELEBRATIONS

These pictures are of the celebrations to mark Queen Victoria's Diamond Jubilee in 1897.

Above: A grand floral archway which was erected at the bottom of Parson Street.

Right: Another floral archway built in the High Street near the entrance to the Tanyard looking east.

STREET CELEBRATIONS

Above: *Crowds throng the street for the Silver Jubilee parade of 1978. The notice on the carrier bike reads: 'I was delivering during coronation year, I was 75 then'. (DC)*

Above: *Porlock Museum's entry for the carnival of 1994. Left to right: John Thorne, Ros Hammond, Cilla Barney. (PM)*

Left: *Start of a pram race to Porlock Weir. (DC)*

STREET CELEBRATIONS

Above: *A restored gipsy caravan takes part in the fun and games of Porlock Carnival, 1994. (GH)*

Below: *Carnival parade for the Silver Jubilee, 1978. W.I. walkers in their colourful robes. (DC)*

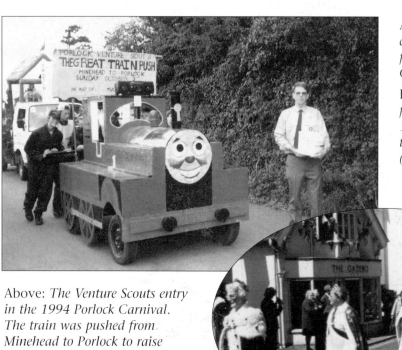

Above: *The Venture Scouts entry in the 1994 Porlock Carnival. The train was pushed from Minehead to Porlock to raise money for a multiple sclerosis appeal. Leader on the right: Graham Haw. (GH)*

FIELD EVENTS

Left: *The Scouts' tug-of-war event, c.1990. This competition was won by the team from Simonsbath – the prize: a barrel of cider. (DC)*

Below: *Sparkhayes camp field on a busy summer's day. (PW)*

Above: *Donkey Derbys were an annual event during the 1960s. (DC)*

Right: *Porlock Horse Show and Katherine Haw riding Toffee. (GH)*

Left: *Just some of those in the line-up for the judging of the beard-growing competition. (DC)*

Top right: *At the Porlock Revels in June 1969, 'Lorna' (Carol Westcott) presents the winner of the beard-growing competition, Michael Ireland, with first prize of an electric razor (which has never been used!). On the right is the town crier, Arthur Cooksley.*

Top: *R.D. Blackmore, author of* Lorna Doone, *the romance first published in 1869.*

Right: *Poster advertising the Revels held on 21 June 1969 to celebrate the centenary of* Lorna Doone.

LORNA DOONE LANDMARKS

Left: *Oare Church where Lorna Doone was shot and wounded by Carver Doone on the day of her marriage to John Ridd. Today the church is somewhat larger than it would have been in Lorna's time, the eastern chancel having only been added in the 19th century.*

Above: *Robbers Bridge is found between Porlock and Oare*

THE OVERLAND LAUNCH

THE OVERLAND LAUNCH
12th January 1999

A "Centenary Re-enactment" of the Lynmouth-Porlock-Porlock Weir Overland Launch.

The epic launch of the Lynmouth Lifeboat "Louisa" occurred January 12th-13th 1899

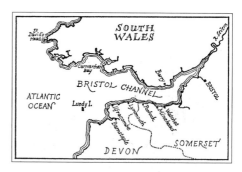

The overland launch re-enactment of January 1999 was staged to celebrate the great event of 1899, when the Lynmouth lifeboat, Louisa, was towed over land to Porlock Weir on the night of 12 January to aid a full-rigged ship, the Forest Hall, *in distress in Porlock Bay. Through appaling weather the RNLI and countless volunteers struggled on to achieve one of the greatest human feats in Porlock's history.*

Below: *Porlock schoolchildren, with the rector, Barry Priory, and teachers, Mrs S. Kevan (head) and Mr J. Patterson, watch the event from behind the church railings.*

THE OVERLAND LAUNCH

Above and right: *The lifeboat makes its way through West Porlock pulled by shire horses. On that stormy night in 1899, some 18 horses were needed to help negotiate the awesome gradients of Countisbury and Porlock hills. They were supplied at not more than an hour's notice, by Mr Jones of Lynton. (Illustration by C.Walter Hodges)*

Left: *The lifeboat arriving at Porlock Weir, 1999. In January 1899, it took ten-and-a-half hours to transport the lifeboat from Lynton to Porlock and she finally launched into the channel at 6.30a.m. on Friday 13th! It was to be more than another ten hours before the lifeboatmen would set foot on dry land again – this time with the crew of the* Forest Hall, *all safely escorted out of danger to the port of Barry, South Wales.*

WASSAILING THE ORCHARD

A photo of c.1910 taken in the orchard in Doverhay, now Orchard Rise. Nearly every village then held a wassailing ceremony on twelfth night to scare off evil spirits and ensure a good crop of cider apples in the coming season. (PM)

IN THE 'GOOD OLD DAYS' THE FARMER USED TO WASSAIL HIS CIDER ORCHARDS
IN BLOSSOM-TIME, AND THE TRADITIONAL SONG STILL SURVIVES:

OLD APPLE TREE, I WASSAIL THEE,
AND HOPE THAT THOU WILT BEAR,
FOR THE LORD DOTH KNOW WHERE WE SHALL BE
TO BE MERRY ANOTHER YEAR.
TO BLOW WELL AND TO BEAR WELL,
AND SO MERRY LET US BE.
LET EVERY MAN DRINK OFF HIS CUP;
HERE'S HEALTH TO THE OLD APPLE TREE.

(SHOUTING CHORUS)

OLD APPLE TREE, I WASSAIL THEE,
AND HOPES THAT THOU WILT BEAR
HATS FULL, CAPS FULL,
THREE BUSHEL BAGS FULL,
TALLAT HOLES FULL,
LITTLE HEAP UNDER THE STAIR,
HIP, HIP, HIP, HURRAH, HURRAH!
GUNS – BANG, BANG, BANG!

Conclusion

Today we all tend to look back with nostalgia to earlier times and old photographs, be they of family or of local views and scenes. We have to thank such people as Francis Frith, one of the early pioneers of the picture postcard and, closer to home, Alfred Vowles, who resided, in his early days, in Porlock, and later in Minehead. Vowles took hundreds of photographs of the area, going to tremendous trouble using heavy equipment and, whilst living in Porlock, developed and printed his shots in his own home, a caravan *(below)*.

Many photographers, both professional and amateur, follow on and produce lovely photographs. We see by these pictures how the scene has changed, but we must remember that everything is changing still and it is for this reason that I, and many others, take photographs in the same area.

I hope that you enjoy *The Book of Porlock* and look forward to making the most of the area in the years to come. The village cannot be kept as a museum as many people have to live and earn a living here and we must remember that nothing in this world is permanent; we only hope that any future change will be for the good of both local residents and those who come to the area for relaxation, retirement or holidays.

Alfred Vowles outside his caravan. (PM)

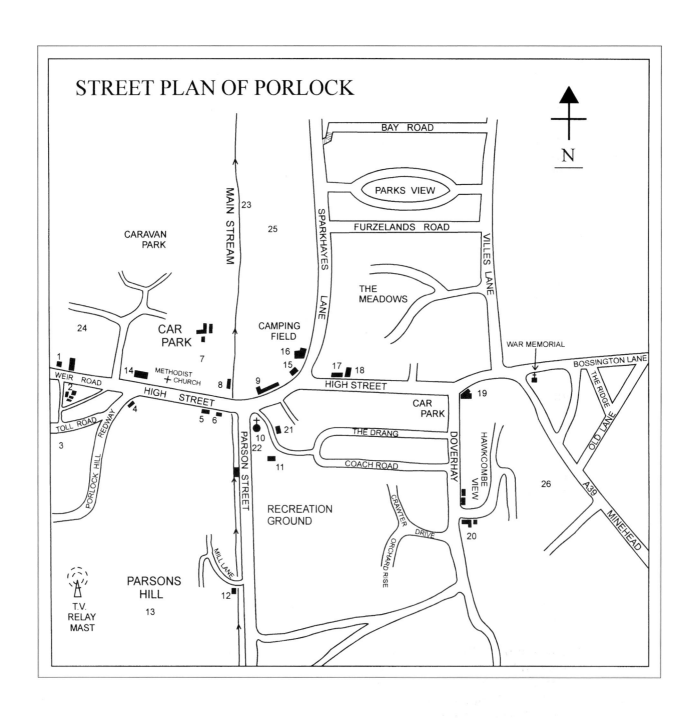

STREET PLAN OF PORLOCK

Map and Plan of Porlock

1. The Pound The Pound was used for holding stray animals and has been used within living memory. The present building was erected after 1844, before which the Pound was on the left of the old entrance to Court Place.

Splat Barn Splat means allotment, so there is possibly some connection with the manor strip system. The house is marked as a building of historic interest on the 6-inch map of 1929.

2. Court Place Court Place is where the lord of the manor lived. In 1420 the Manor House had a hall and a great chamber. In 1640, Gerard writes: 'not farre from the Town you may see an Ancient Manor House'. The house was burnt down in the early 19th century and a new one built on a site nearby. The Manor Court was still being held in 1842.

3. The Parks and Conygar The Parks were useful for keeping pigs. Tenants paid 2d. for 'wood-weyght' (the right to take wood) and 1d. for 'fer-neheu' (the right to take ferns). The 'Coney-garth' or 'Coney-acre' was where the lord of the manor caught his rabbits.

4. Ship Inn In 1797 the Poet Laureat, Robert Southey, stayed at the Ship Inn and wrote the poem beginning 'Porlock, thy verdant vale... '. The coach to Lynmouth stopped there and took on two extra horses, hired from local farmers or traders, to help take the coach up the steep hill.

5. The Castle Inn Once thatched, the old Castle Inn was sold in 1887 for £900 and then demolished to make way for the present Castle Hotel.

6. Town Mill The Manor or Town Mill was sited between Abbeyfield and the Castle Hotel. The 20 customary tenants of 1306 were bound by agreement to clean out the mill pond on Hockday (the second Tuesday after Easter). In the Bailiffs' Rolls of 1419-26 Lady Harrington had to spend much money to keep the mill in repair.

7. The Tannery This was once the home of Porlock's largest industry – the production of leather. The Tanyard is first mentioned in 1794 when it belonged to Abraham Phelps. It closed after the First World War.

8. Market Place The Market Place was the sight of the weekly market as well as two or three annual fairs which were first granted in 1366 and again in 1614. Tradition speaks of a 'beautiful market house', but where it was is not known. There was still a Market Cross in Porlock in 1810. On the Tithe Map of 1844 there is a small building near the Central Garage, parallel to the river, which is called the Market House. Markets disappeared around 1800 but fairs continued until the 1870s.

9. Rose and Crown Inn Only two inns are mentioned in a directory of 1794; the Ship and the Rose and Crown, where it is believed R.D. Blackmore once stayed. In 1870 the landlady was summoned for rowdy behaviour in the Crown, which was closed down about ten years later.

10. The Church of St Dubricius The earliest part of the church dates from the 13th century. It is thought to have been rebuilt by Sir Simon Fitzroges at the beginning of the 14th century and his effigy still stands in the church. St Dubricius was a Welsh saint and it seems very likely that West Somerset was christianised from Wales. The church was probably built on a site once used for pagan worship.

11. The Old Rectory Part of the Old Rectory dates back to the 15th century or earlier. The first Porlock rector was John, son of Rogo, appointed in 1297. Since 1559 the living has been in the gift of the crown. The new Rectory was built in 1992.

12. Hawkcombe or Parsonage Mill This was part of the Rectorial Manor.

13. Parsons Hill So called because it belonged to the Church Manor, the hill is also sometimes referred to as 'Burley'.

14. The Old School The Old School which now houses the Information Centre, the library, the Council Office and the Lovelace Centre, opened in 1876 and was closed when the present school in Parson Street opened in 1993. An earlier school-room was sited in Parson Street and was run by subscription.

15. The Chapel The old chapel was built in 1837 (nearly 30 years after the first Methodist services were held in the village). The new chapel opened in 1927 and the original building is now a café.

16. Sparkhayes Formerly a farm, Sparkhayes was first mentioned in 1383 and once belonged to the Earl of Lovelace.

17. The Three Horse Shoes This building was on the site of the Lorna Doone Hotel and is mentioned in the 1822 Register of Inns.

18. The Royal Oak On the Tithe Map there is an inn next door to the Three Horse Shoes called the Somerset Inn, owned by Abraham Sparks junr. This was probably the Royal Oak.

19. Dovery Court or Manor Now the Museum and Snooker Club, the Court was probably first used as a dower house for the Lady when her husband died. 'An example of a remarkably small Manor house of the fifteenth century', it was restored in 1894, paid for by Sir Charles E.H. Chadwyck-Healey and is now owned by Porlock Parish Council.

20. Doverhay Farms and Inns Both Lower and Higher Doverhay Farms (now no longer worked) were once the homes of substantial yeoman. There were two taverns in Doverhay in 1280, in one of which a man was murdered – the event led to a fine for the entire hundred of Carhampton.

21. The Priests' House – The Harrington Chantry The Harrington memorial in the church is one of the finest of its kind and was erected in memory of Lord and Lady Harrington. The first priest was appointed in 1476 and the Chantry closed in 1546. The priest had to reside 'in a certain messuage, hard by the cemetery of the church' and the chaplains had to provide bread and cheese and ten gallons of good beer to be eaten and drunk in memory of the Lord and Lady after the anniversary service.

22. Houses around the Church These were knocked down in c.1890 and the position of the road altered. There was an archway into the church and it was here that the stocks were kept in the early 19th century. There was a dwelling over the archway and one of the houses was a malt house (one of six in Porlock in the early 1800s).

23. Mesne Stream The Meadowland, the most valued land in the area, was held in common and bordered the stream.

24. The Buttyard This was where archery was practised by order of the king. The field is now covered with bungalows.

25. The Fields In 1306, 20 villeins held a furlong each, in return for many duties to the lord of the manor. The field (i.e. the open field) is frequently mentioned in the Bailiffs' Rolls of 1419-26, but only in connection with haymaking. In 1509 the common fields were called Netherlands, Cowlease, Uppastyle and Pownde Park. There were also Wheatpark, Buttyard, Allerpark and Conygar.

26. Doverhay – Luccombe The separation of Doverhay from Porlock goes back at least to Saxon times. The name is possibly British in origin. Doverhay was joined to Porlock Civil Parish in 1928.

27. The Decoy – Coy Barn Cygnets were taken from the Marsh for the Lady Harrington's table in 1420 – 'the expenses of divers men taking cygnets by order of the Lady; 10d.'

Dovery Manor, which now houses Porlock Museum and the Snooker Club.

Bibliography and Suggested Further Reading

Allen, N.V., *Exmoor Place Names*, Alcombe Books, 1986

Astell, Joan, *Around Minehead*, Alan Sutton Publishing Ltd., n.d.

Binding, Hilary, *Exmoor 40 Years On*, Exmoor Books, 1994

Binding Hilary, *Old Minehead and Around*, Exmoor Books, 1983

Blackmore, R.D., *Lorna Doone*, 1869

Bouquet, M., *No Gallant Ship*, Hollis and Carter, 1959

Chadwych-Healey, C., *The History of Part of West Somerset*, Southeran, Collinson, 1901

Morley, K., *Porlock, West Porlock, Porlock and Culbone*, Cox, n.d.

Corner, Dennis, *Porlock in Those Days*, Halsgrove, 1992

Eales, F.C., *The Church of St Dubricius, Porlock*, Barnicott and Pearce, 1935

Farr, G., *Somerset Harbours*, Christopher Johnson, 1954

Gilman, J., *Nineteenth Century West Somerset Sailing Ships*, unpublished

Halliday, M., *Description of the Monuments and Effigies in Porlock Church*, Torquay, 1882

Hawkins, M. and Grimley, R., *A Century of Coaching on Exmoor*, Exmoor Books, 1998

Hawkins, M., *Somerset at War 1939-1945*, Dovecote Press, 1988

Hodges, C. Walter, *The Overland Launch*, Exmoor Books, 1999

West Somerset Villages in Old Photographs from the Hole Collection, Alan Sutton Publishing Ltd., n.d.

Hook, Rev Walter, M.A., *A History of the Ancient Church of Porlock and of the Patron Saint, St. Dubricius and His Times*, Parker, 1893

Hurley, J., *Exmoor in Wartime 1939-1945*, Exmoor Press, 1978

Marshall, H.J., *Exmoor Sporting and Otherwise*, Eyre and Sottiswoode, 1948

Mold, E.T., 'Culbone Hill Stones', Exmoor Review, 1983

Morris, J. (ed.), *Domesday Book (No.8) Somerset*, Phillimore, 1980

Page, J.L.W., *An Exploration of Exmoor*, Seeley, 1890

Pointon, A.G., *Methodism in West Somerset*, P.P., 1982

Ridler, J.K., *A Selworthy Notebook*, P.P., 1983

Savage, J., *History of the Hundred of Carhampton*, Strong, 1830

Smith, G. *Smuggling in the Bristol Channel 1700-1850*, Countryside Books, 1989

Symons, W., *Early Methodism in West Somerset*, Kelly, 1895

Waters, B., *The Bristol Channel*, Dent, 1955

SUBSCRIBERS

B. A. Adams, Hawkcombe, Porlock, Somerset

Colin J. & Rosemary G. Albon, Bedford

Noel Allen M.B.E., Minehead, Somerset

Miss Liz Anderson, Coombe Wood, Porlock, Somerset

Margaret Anderson, Allerford, Porlock, Somerset

Frederick & Kathleen Archer, Porlock, Somerset

Dorothy A. Arscott, Porlock, Somerset

Jane Bailey, Danbury, Essex

M. Jean Barker (née Berry), Porlock, Somerset

Rev. Linda J. Barriball, Minehead, Somerset

E. F. Barwick, Porlock, Somerset

Mick & Lesley Beard, Wordsley, West Midlands

Don Beeson, Porlock, Somerset

Ruth Bettie (née White), Midlands

Mr H. Binding, Taunton, Somerset

Sylvia & Terry Blackwell, Camberley, Surrey

Rodney Blanthorn, Alcombe, Minehead, Somerset

Elizabeth A. Bodley, Minehead, Somerset

Brian J. Bodley, Minehead, Somerset

Patricia M. Bodman, Porlock, Somerset

Deborah Bolton, Bridgwater, Somerset

Mr & Mrs C. H. Bowden, Porlock, Somerset

David & Ann Britnell, Porlock, Somerset

A. J. P. Bryant, Porlock, Somerset

Mrs Yvonne Bryant, formerly of Porlock, Somerset

Mrs B. E. Bullen, Minehead, Somerset

Tony Burgess, Porlock, Somerset

Mr. E. G. Burgess, Totton, Southampton

G. A. Burrows, Porlock, Somerset

Mrs Julia Burt, Porlock School, Somerset

Mrs S. Butler, Porlock, Somerset

Sir David Calcutt QC, Twitchen, Porlock, Somerset

Mrs Nina Calloway, Alcombe, Minehead, Somerset

Fred Cape, Porlock, Somerset

Peter J. Carter, Bossington Lane, Porlock, Somerset

Keith & Sue Chappell, Porlock, Somerset

Vera L. Charles, Alcombe, Minehead, Somerset

Graham J. Chilman, Nailsworth, Gloucestershire

Richard Clutterbuck, Bristol

Ernest James Cooksley, Porlock, Somerset

Marcus J. Cooksley, Broadway, Ilminster, Somerset

Clare E. Copp, Minehead, Somerset

Robin Court, Minehead, Somerset

Mrs E. P. Cree, Porlock, Somerset

Irene & David Cross, Pitt Farm, Porlock, Somerset

Brian Culcheth, Porlock, Somerset

Dr Peter & Mrs Carole Darke, Bicknoller

Jackie & Derek Dascombe, West Luccombe, Minehead, Somerset

Mr & Mrs J. Davies, Porlock, Somerset

June Davis, Porlock, Somerset

M. E. Davis, Allerford, Minehead, Somerset

Margaret R. Dean, Minehead, Somerset

Angela & Roy Derrick, Porlock, Somerset

Martin H. N. Down, Porlock, Somerset

John Drakeley, Porlock, Somerset

Miss S. H. Duck, Porlock, Somerset

Henry Dyer, West Porlock House, Porlock, Somerset

Sheila & Gerry Eddolls, Porlock, Somerset

David & Susan England, Porlock, Somerset

Isobel & Don Evans, Porlock & Blagdon, Somerset

Margaret Fairlie M.B.E., Porlock, Somerset

Dennis (John) Farmer, Downend, Bristol

Charlotte Farrar, Forge Cottage, Porlock, Somerset

Mr & Mrs R. S. Fitzer (née Sizer), Porlock, Somerset

Ivy & Dennis Fitzgerald

Steve & Chris Fitzgerald, Seapoint, Porlock, Somerset

Michael John Floyd, 'Redway', Porlock, Somerset

Eileen Floyde, Porlock, Somerset

John & Sandie Floyde, Porlock, Somerset

Tim J. P. Forster, Old Rectory, Porlock, Somerset

F. J. Fouracre, Porlock, Somerset

Betty French (née Slade), Norwich, Norfolk

Walter E. H. Fry, Porlock, Somerset

Alan & Yvonne Fry, Darby Green, Blackwater, Hampshire

Rosemarie A. Gande, Luccombe, Somerset

Gail P. Gibbons, Minehead, Somerset

John W. Gibbons, Allerford, Somerset

Caroline Giddens, Minehead, Somerset

Daphne M. Gilham J.P. (née Bryant), Taunton, Somerset

Paul Goldsmith, Porlock, Somerset

Margaret Gould, Dunster, Somerset

U. & A. Gould, Porlock, Somerset

Mr R. Gould, Porlock, Somerset

Mr N. Grandfield, Sampford Peverell, Tiverton, Devon

Mrs Margaret Grantham, West Porlock, Somerset

Philip Griffin, Wootton Courtenay, Minehead, Somerset

Molly E. Groves (née Blunt), Oare, Lynton, Devon

Joan Hadley, Porlock, Somerset

Mrs S. Hall, Porlock, Somerset

A. Hammel, Porlock, Somerset

Mrs R. Hart, Sampford Peverell, Tiverton, Devon

Graham Haw, Horner Mill, Porlock, Somerset

Dr Julian & Mrs Karen Hawkins, Wanborough

Gertrude E. Hawkins (née Bryant), Poole, Dorset

Susan Hester, Porlock, Somerset

Mrs L. Higginbottom, Dulverton, Somerset

Reginald R. Higgins, Porlock, Somerset

Charles Hills, Porlock, Somerset

Donald Hooper, Porlock, Somerset

Mrs Joan Howell, Porlock, Somerset

Claire & Steve Huggins, New Zealand

David J. Huish, Plymouth, Devon

John A. Huish, Porlock, Somerset

Mrs M. J. Hurrell, Porlock, Somerset

Eva & John Hutton, Woodham, Surrey

Michael & Joan Ireland, Porlock, Somerset

Phillip Ireland, Rowlands Castle, Portsmouth, Devon

Graham & Jenny James, Porlock, Somerset

Jill Jenkerson, Fairgarden, Porlock, Somerset

Robert & Ursula Johnson, Porlock, Somerset

SUBSCRIBERS

Eve Johnson, Tiverton, Devon
Danny & Ann Jones, Porlock, Somerset
Mr Alfred Keal, Porlock, Somerset
Sue Kevan, Porlock School, Somerset
Ruby M. Kibby (née Pugsley), Porlock, Somerset
Gordon E. Kidd, Porlock, Somerset
G. M. Kievill, Minehead, Somerset
Rachel Krouwel (née White), Bristol
Nigel & Sue Lamacraft, Porlock, Somerset
Kate Lamacraft
Anne D. Lamacraft, Porlock, Somerset
Callum J. Langley, Porlock, Somerset
Roger Langrish, Wootton Courtenay, Minehead, Somerset
Hugo Langrish, Martock, Somerset
David & Jackie Latham, Porlock, Somerset
Ann Lee (née Sizer), Arizona, U.S.A.
Adrian J. Locke, London N17
Julian C. Locke, London N17
Joan Loraine, Porlock, Somerset
J. Luke, Minehead, Somerset
Gillian M. Malyon (née Pollard), Cheltenham, Glos.
Malcolm McCoy, Hawkcombe, Porlock, Somerset
Helen McKay, Porlock, Somerset
N. V. Meachem, Porlock, Somerset
Sheila M. Medlam, Porlock, Somerset
Gwendoline Middleton, Porlock, Somerset
Mr & Mrs Derek J. Miles, Porlock, Somerset
Monty & Elsa Montagu, Cape Town, South Africa
Kenneth J. Moore, Timberscombe, Somerset
John Moore, Porlock, Somerset
Kay Morton, Porlock, Somerset
Mrs Mary Norton, Wootton Courtenay, Minehead, Somerset
Kathy Nott, Minehead, Somerset
Hugh Owen, Prague
William Owen, Wiltshire
J. Ann Paterson (née Pearce), Porlock, Somerset
Carole Pearse, Minehead, Somerset
David Pearson & Shelley Beard, Coseley, West Midlands
Susan Peel (née Burgess), Great Bedwyn, Wiltshire
Jack Percival, Marlow, Bucks.
Laurie Perkins, Porlock, Somerset
Mrs L. Perkins, Minehead, Somerset
Lynne & Viv Perkins
Margaret & Edgar Perkins
Vivian & Molly Perkins, Porlock, Somerset
Ray Perkins, Haslemere, Surrey

Michael Plenty, Minehead, Somerset
Mr Paul H. Pollard, Lyneham, Chippenham, Wiltshire
Victor Charles Poppy, Carhampton, Somerset
Michael Prideaux & Kathy Bickerstaff, Higher Allerford, Minehead, Somerset
Edna H. Pritchard, Minehead, Somerset
Graham & Joy Pugsley, Clevedon, Somerset
Margaret A. Pugsley (née Pollard), Porlock, Somerset
Mia & John Purvis, Taunton, Somerset
Lyn & Derek Purvis, Porlock, Somerset
Emma & Philip Purvis, Taunton, Somerset
David & Angela Rawle, Minehead, Somerset
George G. Read, Bristol
Dr David Redston, Bristol
Iris M. Redston (née Bray), Minehead, Somerset
Tony Reed, Porlock, Somerset
George J. Reynolds, Minehead, Somerset
Alexandra L. Rice, Bath
Anthony J. Richards, Porlock, Somerset
Richard G. Richards, Porlock, Somerset
W. D. Richards, Porlock, Somerset
Miles & Rosalind Robertson, Frinton-on-Sea, Essex/Porlock, Somerset
John C. Robins, North Newton, Bridgwater, Somerset
Richard J. Robins, Bossington, Somerset
Veronica Ross, Minehead, Somerset
Mr Eric Rowlands, Luccombe, Minehead, Somerset
Nick Russell, Wellington, New Zealand
John Russell, Porlock, Somerset
Joan Avery Rutt (née Corner), Coventry
Mrs E. & Mr C. Sage, Porlock, Somerset
Mr & Mrs Malcolm Sage, Porlock, Somerset
Betty J. Savage, Porlock, Somerset
Malcolm Scott, Minehead, Somerset
Dr D. S. Sharpe, Porlock, Somerset
Peter & Daphne Sims, Porlock, Somerset
Mr & Mrs G.P. Sizer, Minehead, Somerset
Mr & Mrs D. N. Sizer, Taunton, Somerset
J. M. Skudder, Doniford, Somerset

John H. Smith, Mitcham, Surrey
John Sparks, Porlock, Somerset
Barbara Starr (née Ley), Porlock Weir, Somerset
June & Travers Stiles-Cox, Porlock, Somerset
Miss C. H. Stroud, Bournemouth, Dorset
Steven L. Sully, Minehead, Somerset
Raymond J. Sully, Baltimore, U.S.A.
Peter & Sheila Sutton, Hawkcombe, Porlock, Somerset
Martin R. Sutton, Walberton, Arundel, Sussex
David J. Tancock, Alcombe, Minehead, Somerset
Mr L. Tancock, Porlock, Somerset
Brenda & Gilbert Tancock
Henry J. Taylor, Porlock, Somerset
R. A. S. Taylor, Langton Herring, Weymouth, Dorset
Vivienne Taylor & David Young, Porlock, Somerset
John Thorne, Porlock, Somerset
Anne Tomalin (née Slade), Fleet, Hants.
Bobby Vallance, Porlock, Somerset
Richard Vaughan, Porlock, Somerset
Terence D. Walker, Porlock, Somerset
Marie & Julian Walters, Long Load
Pam Ward, Hawkcombe, Porlock, Somerset
Brian Watson-Harrison, Porlock, Somerset
Mr M. K. Watts, Porlock, Somerset
M. A. Wells, Hawkcombe, Porlock, Somerset
Lesley Wells, Porlock, Somerset
Susan Westwood, New Mexico, U.S.A.
Andrew White, Bristol
Richard White, Peterborough, Cambs.
Mabel Whitmarsh, Porlock, Somerset
Glyn & Gwen Willicombe, Porlock, Somerset
Marjorie M. Wilson, Porlock, Somerset
James H. Wood, Porlock, Somerset
Dr. Andrew Woodcock, Uckfield, East Sussex
Tony Woods, Allerford, Minehead, Somerset
Martyn & Sally Wright, East Garston, Berkshire
David & Mea Wright, Porlock, Somerset
C. H. E. Wright, Porlock, Somerset
D. A. Wyatt, Porlock, Somerset
Rev. George H. Yates, Poole, Dorset

Also available in the Community History Series:

Further information:

If you would like to order a book or find out more about having your parish featured in this series,
please contact The Editor, Community History Series, Halsgrove House, Lower Moor Way, Tiverton
Business Park, Tiverton, Devon, EX16 6SS, tel: 01884 243242 or visit us at http://www.halsgrove.com
If you are interested in a particular photograph in this volume, it may be possible to supply you
with a copy of the image.

The Doverhay, Porlock.